www.nononsenseguides.com

The No Nonsense Creed

The best way to go fly fishing is to find out a little something about a water, and then just go. Trying, figuring, wrong turns, surprises, self-reliance and discovering something new, even in familiar waters, are what make the memories.

The next best way is to learn enough from a local to save you from going too far wrong. You'll still find the water on your own, and it still feels as if you were the first.

This is the idea for our unique No Nonsense fly fishing series. Our books reveal little hush-hush information, yet they give all you need to find what will become your own secret places.

Painstakingly pared down, our writing is elegantly simple. Each title offers a local fly fishing expert's candid tour of favorite fly fishing waters. Nothing is over-sold or out of proportion. Everything is authentic, especially the discoveries and experiences you get after using our books.

No Nonsense Fly Fishing Guidebooks give you a quick, clear, understanding of the essential information needed to fly fish a region's most outstanding waters. The authors are highly experienced and qualified local fly fishers. Maps are tidy versions of the author's sketches.

About the Cover

The cover painting is by outdoor artist Dan Rickards. Titled *Late For Dinner*, the fly fisherman is casting to the "Cabin Hole" on the Metolius river, just upstream from the Camp Sherman Bridge.

Dan lives in Sisters, Oregon with his wife and four children on their ten-acre ranch. He began his career as a full-time professional artist in 1991 and has been widely recognized and acclaimed for his fishing, hunting and outdoor art. See more of Dan Rickards' fly fishing artwork at his gallery in Sisters, Oregon and at www.nononsenseguides.com.

About These Books

The publisher is located in the tiny Western town of Sisters, Oregon, just a few miles from the Metolius River. A couple of fly fishers create No Nonsense books, including Pete Chadwell who does all the layout, illustrations and maps. This work is a testament to his accuracy and desire to get out and fly fish new waters.

All who produce these books believe in providing top quality products at reasonable prices. We also believe all information should be confirmed whenever possible. We never hesitate to go out, fly rod in hand, to verify the facts and figures that appear in the pages of our books. The staff is committed to this grueling research. It's dirty work, but we're glad to do it for you.

For more on No Nonsense Fly Fishing Guidebooks, our authors, and some neat fly fishing stuff, visit www.nononsenseguides.com.

Seasons of the Metolius

Seasons of the Metolius

The Life of a River Seen Through the Eyes of a Fly Fisherman

John Judy

Illustrated by Pete Chadwell

Seasons of the Metolius
The Life of a River, Seen Through The Eyes of A Fly Fisherman
ISBN #1-892469-11-1

© 2002 No Nonsense Fly Fishing Guidebooks
Published by No Nonsense Fly Fishing Guidebooks
Sisters, Oregon 97759 www.nononsenseguides.com

Author: John Judy
Editors: David Banks, Helen Condon
Maps, Illustrations & Production: Pete Chadwell
Fold-Out Map: Charley Engle, Pete Chadwell
Fold-Out Photos: John Judy, Guido Raha
Cover Artwork: Dan Rickards
Back Cover Photos: John Judy, David Banks
Printed by Hignell Book Printing
488 Burnell Street
Winnipeg, Manitoba, Canada R3G 2B4

Disclaimer: While this guide will greatly help readers to fly fish, it is not a substitute for caution, good judgment and the services of a qualified fly fishing guide or outfitter.

In memory of Michael Leitheiser,
a good friend of the Metolius.

Table of Contents

Foreword

OK, I lied a little, placing our No Nonsense logo on this book, but I did not mean to deceive.

Our No Nonsense Fly Fishing Guidebooks provide essential information on where to fly fish. We do this with detailed maps and without a lot wasted motion, or "falderal" as our original author Harry Teel put it.

Seasons of the Metolius, by John Judy, does provide fly fishing location information, but it mostly describes the natural history of the place. Admittedly, this takes more words than our other guidebooks.

A hallmark of our titles, though, is well-organized, concise information. John's work falls right in line and is a smallish book, partly because of his precise, well chosen words. In short form John has condensed many, many years of observation, thought, conservation action, study, newspaper columns, photography, and fly fishing. His eloquence paints a handsome picture that frees one's imagination to in-fill with still richer splendor. This book embodies our No Nonsense idea of parsimony and then takes it to a new, artful level. It is our first in this regard.

To honorably live up to our creed, we include some helpful "where to" fly fishing information and maps in the back of this book. We hope you have a chance to fish the Metolius, or the other easily accessed places we've outlined. After all, if you are even a tiny bit disposed to try fly fishing, reading *Seasons of the Metolius* will probably make you want to get to it. If fly fishing isn't of interest, these spots are also beautiful places to hike, picnic, camp, (run into John Judy) or simply sit and watch. If you go, I suggest you take notes. Who knows, after thirty years maybe you'll have a book too.

David Banks
Sisters, Oregon
May 2002

1
A Mountain Valley

FATE'S SEAL

I slammed my fist on the stamp. "Done!" Over sixty copies of my resumé typed and ready for the mail, each one hand done. In those days, before computers, you couldn't use copies. Employers expected to see freshly typed originals and while typing the last half dozen I had been itching to be finished. There was an excellent hatch on a nearby river and I wanted to be there. Now at last I was done and, with a clear conscience, I could go fishing.

My old Irish Setter, Sterling, met me at the door. Like most of her breed, Sterling was a free spirit and somewhere along the line she had gotten a couple of wires crossed. She didn't know she was supposed to be a bird dog, she thought her role in life was fish dog and she was good at it, too. She heard the faint sound of my rod rattling in the tube, from inside the house, while she was napping outside in the sun. She was there at the door ready to greet me, going around in circles in the classic hyper red dog style. She knew we were going out.

"Get out of the way, you goofy mutt," I warned. I kicked at her half-heartedly not really intending to hit her at all. I was loaded down with my fishing rod, waders and vest, plus all the resumés which I was going to drop off at the mailbox on the way out. I was having a little trouble with the door when the dog hit me in the back of the knees. I juggled everything for a second and, by some miracle, only one letter went down. Sterling stomped on it immediately with a muddy paw.

I picked the letter up, brushed the dirt off and looked at it. It was addressed to a little ski area out in Oregon. If I were to take that job I'd be living in a town called Camp Sherman. There was a river there with a funny name, the Metolius (I had all these jobs catalogued by fish potential). I had heard about that river, read an article or something. It was supposed to be good.

For a minute, I thought about taking the envelope back and changing it. Then I looked at my load, looked at the dog, and thought about how badly I wanted to be outside fishing. That was it, my fate was sealed with the dog's stamp of approval. Of course, the muddy paw print got me the job.

THE TALL TREES

My first time in Central Oregon was when I drove out for the job interview. Coming in from the east on Highway 20, I could see the mountains and the forest from a long ways out. As you drive across the sagebrush and juniper plains of the high desert, the mountains are there in front of you, beckoning. You see a large section of the Cascades from Mount Hood, south. There are more than half a dozen major snow capped peaks, but Black Butte is the sentinel that guides you in, it's the spot on the map that marks your destination.

The Butte is an enormous cinder cone, a perfectly symmetrical little volcano that has pushed up some three thousand feet out of the plains. It sits just a few miles east of the main north-south line of the Cascades, and the road to Camp Sherman goes right around the base of it. Its slopes are covered with timber except for the very top where it almost stretches high enough to go above the tree line. As you drive in, it becomes larger and larger and then suddenly, about ten miles out in the little town of Sisters, you go into the trees and lose the view.

The transition from desert to trees is very abrupt because the Cascades create an enormous rain shadow. Storms push in off the Pacific Ocean and climb the steep west side of the mountains. Huge amounts of water are squeezed from the clouds as they climb in elevation. This is the mossy, wet, timbered side of Oregon that everybody knows. As soon as the storms top over the ridge the energy is dissipated and with every mile you travel towards the east the annual rain and snow fall amounts drop dramatically. At the crest of the Cascades in the winter, there's snow fifteen and twenty feet deep. Just a few miles further on, there's so little moisture that trees won't grow. The sagebrush and juniper of the high desert is the side of Oregon not so many people are aware of.

As I drove through the transition zone, the size of the trees increased rapidly. When I came around the south side of the Butte, I ran into the first of the big, old-growth Ponderosa pines. For someone unaccustomed to the great forests of the Pacific Northwest these are not just big trees, they are spectacular. But it's not just size alone that makes the Ponderosas special; it's their appearance, too. The bark is cracked and split. Up close, the flakes look like little puzzle pieces but from a distance it's a very pleasing pattern of reddish brown on tan. They are very striking, very dramatic trees, especially in the fading sunlight. As I turned down the road into Camp Sherman, I drove through a corridor of these giants. My car slowed and my head turned. I was already starting to feel the magic of the Metolius and I hadn't even seen the river yet.

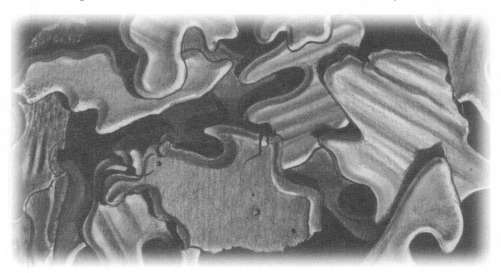

A TOUR OF THE MAP

Because the valley is forested, it's sometimes difficult to get a handle on the lay of the land inside the basin. There aren't very many places you can go to get a clear overview. The map included with this book gives a unique and interesting perspective. In this view, all of the major land features are easily distinguished. Unfold it and let me take you on a tour.

Black Butte is the sentinel at the south entrance to the valley. From the ground, it's the dominant feature of the landscape, but on the map it doesn't seem quite as important because it's dwarfed a bit by the appearance of Green Ridge. The ridge and the butte are companion features of the geography. One sits vertically and the other horizontally. Even though the wall of the ridge is a large and important land feature, from the ground its size and structure are difficult to appreciate. You see it only in filtered views through the trees so you don't get a full impression of its length and breadth.

Green Ridge is an enormous piece of real estate twenty miles long and ten miles deep. It's a giant uplift, a single block of earth that was tilted up out of the ground at one time by forces I can't even comprehend. If you look eastward off the ridge, it slopes gently away out onto the high desert. On the west side, you're looking down the fractured edge of the fault block, some 2,000 feet sharply down into the valley floor. This escarpment creates the eastern wall of the basin.

The main valley floor, which is about five miles wide, is a continuation of the plain from which both Black Butte and Green Ridge have been uplifted. The other side of the valley is formed by the Cascades. There are two main snow capped peaks. The smaller one, to the south, is Three Finger Jack. Further north, the larger peak is Mount Jefferson, named for the U.S. President that sent Lewis and Clark off to explore the continent.

Streaming off the south side of Mount Jefferson and running down into the valley floor there is the large scar of a fairly recent lava flow. It's a very distinct feature on the map, a clear reminder of the raw and turbulent geology of the region. It's also the southern boundary of the Warm Springs Indian reservation. Everything from the lava flow north along the west side of the river is tribal land.

The Metolius starts right at the base of Black Butte. It comes from a single spring as a full-blown river flowing right out from under the edge of the mountain. According to Indian legend, a very sad mountain spirit, Black Butte, shed a lonely teardrop to make the river.

From the head spring, the river flows north along the base of Green Ridge. After a few miles, it passes through Camp Sherman. This is the town center for this little region but it is not much of a town. It consists of a post office, general store, restaurant, a few cabins and a very fine, little one-room school. There's not much to it and most people like it that way.

As the river continues, there are numerous springs and tributary streams along the way. The basin drains a vast section of the Cascades from the Santiam Pass, just south of Three Finger Jack, all the way to the north side of Mount Jefferson. There's a lot of water being carried away so the river grows very rapidly. Near the headspring, the Metolius is a fairly small, manageable stream that is easy to wade and traverse. It quickly turns into a powerful whitewater river that may only let you get a few feet from the bank in selected places.

Toward the north end of the valley, where the lava flow enters, the river constricts and increases in speed and begins to dig a deep canyon. Beyond this point there are no roads; access is by foot, mountain bike or whitewater raft. The river continues north for a few miles before it bends sharply eastward around the end of Green Ridge. This area is known as the Horn of the Metolius, a very wild and remote region.

This downstream wilderness is kind of an odd arrangement, creating a curious backward form of development and use. Most streams are accessed from the lower reaches upward with the headwaters somewhere high and remote in the mountains. The Metolius, on the other hand, is primarily accessed from the top and flows away into the wilderness. I'm sure this pattern has some impacts that have never been documented.

Once the stream has rounded the horn and started its journey eastward it flows quickly down to the junction with Lake Billy Chinook. Right at the lake the trees turn to sagebrush and the river flows out into the high desert. Before the dam was built, it used to flow another twenty miles all the way down to connect with the main stream of the Deschutes River, but now it stops short. Overall it is a small, compact river, only 29 miles in length, but it's an amazing wild valley, full of the majesty and power of the great Northwest.

WONDERS AND DELIGHTS

The isolation of the region coupled with the transitioning climate has created a melting pot for all kinds of plant and animal species within the valley. It's as if there are little islands of habitat throughout the basin. In one spot, you can have a micro-climate that favors wet, west side plant species. Not far away, on a south slope, there will be only high desert plants. This means a blooming rhododendron may grow within a few hundred yards of a lowly sagebrush. It's a complex, highly interactive environment.

A butterfly collector friend of mine once told me he could capture almost every species known in Oregon right in the Metolius Basin. He knew of no other place like it. He had a cabin here so he could go out and document this single, unique aspect of the region. The butterfly collector's interest only touches the tip of the iceberg. The phenomenon is widespread across most plant and animal species in the valley. The Metolius Basin is a wonderful mixing pot, a hot bed of interesting biological and geological phenomena. They say it was once considered as a possible site for a national park. There is certainly enough to keep a curious person entertained for a long, long time.

The river is the crown jewel of this spectacular landscape. Clear and clean, it flows through the forest and the giant trees like something out of a picture book. There are occasional views out to the mountains; sometimes it's almost too pretty to be real. The scene at the headspring makes a perfect post card picture. The river flows out across a mountain meadow, in the background the snow-covered peak of Mount Jefferson is framed by the tall Ponderosa pines.

EVENING ON THE WATER

My first night in Camp Sherman, I pitched my tent on a point where the river makes a big horseshoe bend. There was water on three sides. It was great to sleep listening to the sounds of the river. That evening I went out to explore a little bit with my fishing rod. It was late May, there had been storms in the mountains and it looked like there could be more rain later. The clouds were scudding fast and low. Everything along the river was washed clean by the rain and the plants were bursting with vitality and new life. There were insect hatches everywhere. I saw the bugs fluttering like snowflakes out over the river corridor where there was plenty of food for fish.

While I was watching for signs of a rising trout, a small wren came out of the bushes and flew out over the river. It hovered wingtip to wingtip with a large caddis, then reached out and took the bug. The performance was repeated again and again. "It must be quite a food source," I thought to myself. It seemed very unusual for a land-based bird like a wren to adapt to a largely aquatic food source as a primary diet. Later on I found the wren's nest and looked in at her new young chicks, bald, mouths agape. She had located her nest well and her young chicks were begging for all that she could supply.

Toward the end of the day, the clouds broke up a little bit and there were some nice colors in the sunset which were reflected off the water. They were also caught by the swirling current of the river to make a kaleidoscope of liquid color. Just then, a large buck came out of the woods on the other side of the river. His horns were in velvet. He stood for a moment, majestically silhouetted against the dark background of the forest and the trees. Then he turned and was gone.

I didn't catch any fish that evening. I didn't even see one rise, but I had a whole new outlook on the job interview. The river had touched me, I wanted to be hired by that little ski area in the worst possible way.

2
The River's Challenge

THE PREDATOR'S EYE

When the job came through, the Metolius became my home river. For almost 25 years since then it has been my great pleasure to try to unravel the secrets of the river. I like trying to understand it, I like seeking out those things that escape the casual eye. I am not a scientist or researcher, just a curious passer-by. Exploring the river is my hobby, my way of coming in touch with the natural world around me.

The Metolius is a small, separate universe all its own; a semi-contained ecosystem which we can neither enter nor ever fully understand. There's another world beneath those rushing currents, an aquatic land which we learn about through hints and clues, by the smallest bits of insight.

My method of observation is to walk the stream with my fly rod in my hand. Through the predator's eye of a man stalking a trout, my senses are heightened, the river is seen in greater detail and with a more subtle nuance. If I were a back-packer, a painter or a photographer, it would not be the same.

The predator role is important; predators are the seers, though we don't always appreciate them as such. In our modern world, with our comfortable detachment from our own food supply, we have a tendency to vilify the predator, to look at him as evil and nasty. In truth the hawk, the eagle, and the coyote are all wonderful animals, known for their vision and keen sight. It is these qualities I wish to emulate and bring to my own exploration.

I try to be a friendly predator, if such a thing is possible. Like most good fly fishermen I practice catch and release and do all that I can to see to the health of the stream and all of its occupants. I still recognize my role though, and am not entirely the fish's friend.

WINDOWS OF INSIGHT

Understanding a complex river is not always easy; enlightening moments can come and go quite quickly. They are like the ebb and flow of the river's current. As you stare deep into a pool trying to see what is hidden there, the shifting currents distort the surface. It's like looking through a moving lens that never quite comes into focus. You see, but you don't see. Weeds and rocks take on life, fish become invisible. Then comes a window, a flat spot in the current, a place where, for a split second, you can see clearly. In that brief moment you see the broad, speckled back of a native rainbow as if it were in a photograph. After that, your perception is changed.

As I approach the Metolius, I come prepared to spend many hours staring into the shifting currents. This is an extremely complex natural environment, far more confounding than the average river. Clues about it come grudgingly. Perhaps it is a single ray of sunlight that shines through the pines in just the right way to show a school of fish clustered at the head of the pool, almost in the rapids, in a place so swift you would not think they could survive. Or maybe it is the shimmering wing of a mayfly spinner that catches the last light of the setting sun and shows you what those mysterious rising trout have been eating.

On many days there will be no insight at all. Nature is not something you can force; it will reveal itself in its own time. You must learn to accept whatever the day will bring. Go forward with child-like wonder in your eye. Poke and probe and explore. Learn to enjoy the search rather than the fruits of the labor. Only then will you really be in a position to appreciate what this grand mistress of a river has to offer.

SPRING WATER

Much of the complexity of the Metolius stems from the fact that it is a spring river. The majority of the flow comes from underground spring sources rather than overland run off. The term spring river is important to fly fishermen. It symbolizes the best of the best. Spring rivers are naturally productive habitats well known for their richness and diversity.

A classic freestone river, an overland flow stream, is an ever-changing habitat. The shores and gravel bars are de-watered during one part of the season and flooded during another. In textbooks, these rivers are characterized by their open, empty gravel bars. Most of the river is only temporary habitat. Fish and insect populations are limited to the size of the stream at its lowest flow.

A spring river, on the other hand, is always full to the banks. Even at the end of a long, hot summer there is plenty of water. Populations of aquatic animals, both fish and insects, are not required to continually move and adjust. Plant communities can grow to the river's edge. This creates an enormous biomass occupying the entire river corridor, both the wetted surface and the associated stream bank.

Stable temperature is another benefit. A river like the Metolius, which comes from the head spring at a very even 48°F year round, may seem freezing cold to someone who is wet wading on a mid-summer day, but it will feel warm on a frosty night in the middle of winter. The cold-blooded fish stay more active, feeding and growing throughout the season. When biologists take scale samples and read them (much as you would read rings on a tree) there is no winter growth check. The river is almost like a hatchery pond where the fish feed and grow all year long.

Spring rivers are nutrient-rich, too. Rainwater, as it falls from the sky, has a slightly acid pH. (This is a naturally occurring condition not to be confused with acid rain.) After this slightly acid water is absorbed into the ground it comes in contact with soils and leaches out valuable nutrients. When it resurfaces as spring water, it is slightly alkaline and carries the necessary foods to stimulate plant growth.

The plants are the beginning of a food web. The plants feed insects, the insects feed fish and the fish feed higher orders of animals like herons, otters, and osprey. In the end, all wild things, plants and animals alike, benefit from the richness and productivity of the spring river environment.

SPRING GEOLOGY

I'm delighted every time I find a new feeder spring to the Metolius. There are hundreds of them, some large, some small. Many are hidden on private land, others surface miles away from the river.

They are often found in beautiful little sylvan grottos tucked away in the forest. Some are unique and mysterious. I know one, the Boiling Spring, that wells up through sand and makes it look as if the ground is boiling. Another, Sugar Spring, is a small waterfall. It appears out of solid rock about fifteen feet above the river and tumbles down through the mossy rocks to the main stream. On occasion, I have gone out and sat in my waders in the middle of this spring and poked my fingers in the holes where the water comes out. I have watched the caddis, flying up-river, make a wrong turn and try to nest in the spring. It's like sitting in the life-blood of the river.

All these springs start in the mountains to the west of the valley, created by the region's volcanic geology. The cinder soil is extremely porous; as the winter snows melt, the run-off is absorbed almost instantly. In June or July, at the base of a snowfield high in the mountains, you can see a small creek emerge from under the snow and then disappear into dusty nothingness in less than 100 yards as it tries to cross the thirsty landscape.

Once absorbed into the soil, this water travels eastward through hidden subterranean pathways until it eventually encounters the Green Ridge up-lift. When the underground water encounters the fault block, it is forced back to the surface and the springs of the Metolius valley are formed.

Right in the spring mouth you can see a food web beginning. The plants often completely overgrow the springs, creating little water gardens. The web rapidly increases in size and complexity. As the spring trickles down to the river, wildflowers grow up along its banks. If you look closely under all the greenery, you'll find an insect colony forming and maybe even a trout minnow or two. Out of even the tiniest upwelling, a unique and wonderful ecosystem is being formed.

NATIVE FISH

It wouldn't be right if a river as interesting and unusual as the Metolius didn't have fish to match. The local native redside rainbow is a remarkable animal. It tends to be greenish gold over the back with a brilliant red/orange side stripe. In the sunlight these colors shimmer and shift. It truly is a living rainbow.

The larger specimens are eighteen or nineteen inches long. On occasion I have seen a few that were even bigger. They are thick, girthy fish, heavy for their length. In your hand they feel muscular and solid. They are so unusual, so visually distinct, that I can still remember the first time I caught one. I didn't know what it was. My education, from back east, had been largely with hatchery-reared rainbow trout. This fish was so unique I could hardly believe it was the same species. I had to examine it in minute detail to be sure.

The capture of that trout, so many years ago, was the beginning of what has become a life-long fascination with native fishes. Eventually, I learned these trout are a uniquely adapted strain. They come from a broader grouping of rainbows, found throughout the Northwest, known as redband trout. Through the evolutionary process, they have developed both appearances and behaviors that make them genetically distinct. Biologists can track key chromosomes in order to make clear determinations of origin. Experienced fishermen can tell on sight. They are unlike any other fish; they are Metolius rainbows.

These native trout are in perfect harmony with their native river. Every aspect of their behavior and appearance from feeding, to spawning, to their distinct rainbow colors, is designed to help them survive in their home river. Their entire life history helps them evade predators like you and me. I've been fooled by them so often that I no longer make assumptions – I don't trust my own eyes. I chuckle when I hear another angler say, "I didn't see a thing," as if that means there is no possibility that a big fat native might be right there in front of him, hiding in plain sight.

It's too bad there are not more native fish in other streams around the country. Our legacy as fishermen and fish managers has not been very good in that regard. In the late 1800's and early 1900's, it was thought that a fish, was a fish, was a fish. The impact of what we were doing was not well understood so, when anglers were unhappy either with the quality or type of fish they were catching, managers were quick to try to improve the situation with planted trout.

Between this invasion of transplanted fishes and the degradation of habitat, native trout have not done all that well. In most parts of the country they are all but gone. On the east coast, native brook trout, which were the prime species in almost all the streams, can only be found in little headwaters creeks. In the Rocky Mountain west, native cutthroats are rare. Almost all the popular fisheries contain either brown trout or rainbows – species that didn't exist in those areas much before the turn of the last century.

While some would argue that I am splitting hairs, that non-native fish left to go wild are every bit as good as native fish in their native habit, I would beg to differ. I have experienced rivers where native and non-native fish of the same species were present. Even when the non-natives were allowed to gain conditioning, they were distinct from the resident fish. An angler could tell which one was which by their strength, by how they fought on the end of a line.

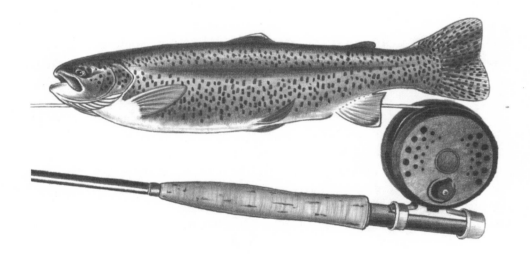

We can tinker and play. We create very good fisheries in places where natives have been lost, but we cannot ever recreate what nature and the process of natural selection has done for us. Wherever they can be found, native fish in native habitat should be treated with special regard. There are not many places like that left in North America. It's a privilege to have it here on the Metolius. It's special, very special, indeed. Feel honored when you feel challenged; you are casting to a unique and wonderful fish when you cast to a Metolius native rainbow.

A MYSTICAL RIVER

With so many biological and geological phenomena locked into one tiny region, it is small wonder the Metolius has become one of the most studied rivers in the state of Oregon. Scientists have been attempting, for years, to quantify, qualify, or otherwise pigeon-hole it into one niche or another. Their attempts have not always been successful. Granted, the research has advanced our understanding and moved us to new perceptions. It has made us aware of aspects of the Metolius we might not have otherwise seen, but in terms of ultimately defining the river, it has fallen well short. Through the scientific eye, we see the river in bits and pieces: we look at the native fish and understand their uniqueness, or we see the springs and understand how they affect the chemical makeup of the water itself. We learn about plants and habitat structures, we see and understand the spawning – where it occurs and when – but none of these things really are the river, they're only part of the whole. No dry scientific text could ever do justice to the reality of the Metolius.

It isn't until you feel the river that you really come to know it. The parts, the pieces, the scientific phenomena, make a whole that seems to have a life of its own. It's as if the river is an entity in itself. If you fish here long enough you will almost certainly be touched by this spirit. Some people say the place has an Indian spirit. I don't know if I believe in such things myself, but I do know that in certain places the land can affect you most profoundly. The Metolius basin is a place that does that.

Because of this spirituality, those who call themselves friends of the river are usually quite fanatical about it. The push for preservation and protection is enormous. Governing agencies like the Forest Service and the Department of Fish and Wildlife know that they must tread lightly here. All of the planning and management reflects the concerns of the people who have felt the spirit of the river.

I find I get closest to this mystical side when I am fishing alone. I remember one day in late spring; the season was turning toward summer and the temperature was pushing into the 90's. In the early afternoon a thundershower passed through. After that, the weather was unsettled. With all the changes, the fish, with their little pressure-sensitive air bladders, didn't know what to make of it – they went crazy. It was a rare mood, but the river wasn't done yet.

The cool air from the snow-capped mountains to the west began to mix with the heat of the high desert to the east. There were alternating pockets of warm and cold air passing through, the temperature was going up and down five or ten degrees in a matter of seconds. The air cells were so distinct you could actually stop and back up a few steps to walk in and out of them.

The pockets of air, drifting over the water, were fed by the moisture of the storm. Vapors began to lift and swirl. Then, quite suddenly, a ghost fog materialized. The changing temperature condensed the moisture in the air; in an instant a pocket of mist appeared in an alcove of the forest. It hovered and swirled for a few minutes like some ghostly spirit until the temperatures changed again and the vapors were re-absorbed; the fog disappeared into thin air just as quickly as it had come. The mood turned from odd to eerie.

The Metolius is like that, always beautiful, but sometimes quite dark and somber, even a little frightening. I could feel the hair on the back of my neck tingling from it. No question the "spirit" was quite tangibly present.

3
Late Winter Dry Flies

THE NYMPHS ARE STIRRING

In the late winter, mayfly nymphs start stirring. It takes just the right light conditions to get them going. The sun has to arrive at a certain point above the horizon and there must be a pre-determined number of days of solar input. When these conditions are met, the insects start migrating along the river-bottom in anticipation of the hatch.

At the first hint of warmth, fishermen start migrating too. I can count on this "pre-hatch" beginning right around the 15th of February. By no means is winter over, but the days are getting a little longer, the weather a bit warmer. My phone will ring. It's some crusty old hard shell who has been dormant under a rock all winter. "Hey, how's fishing going out your way?" The phone never rings just once, the migrating urge spreads quickly throughout the colony. I'll get half-a-dozen calls within a one or two week period. Fishing friends with whom I have not spoken all winter are starting to stir.

The next phase of the hatch is the rise and fall back. The nymphs are building gas pressure underneath their shells. They'll let go and drift toward the surface only to fall back. About this time, license sales in the fly shops shoot up. "Better get legal for this year," they say. Customers begin to finger the rods and eyeball the waders.

If the sunshine continues, the first winged adult mayflies soon begin to appear on the river. A few scattered trout will start feeding and a few cabin-bound fishermen will don their waders and shake the kinks out of unused fly lines.

Hatches and Bugs

Fly fishermen are kind of crazy about insects; they study them and talk about them all the time. An outsider might wonder why, but once you have seen the hatch cycles in action it's easier to comprehend. Insects are like cattle; they convert plant material into animal protein. One of their functions, in the natural scheme of things, is to feed higher orders like birds and fishes. There's an interrelationship, a symbiosis. Like wolves following the caribou, the fish follow the insects. Once you start to understand the broader behavior and life-cycle patterns of insects, it elevates you from a random caster to a more intelligent fisherman who is at least trying to understand and interact.

All of the study culminates in the hatch, when a number of insects appear on the water at same time. They do this for a couple of reasons. By swarming, the winged adults can be sure they will find a mate, but they also swarm as a form of protection, a way to run the gauntlet of predators that are all around. If the insects emerge in large numbers, the fish and birds can't get them all, so while many will be eaten, enough get through to assure survival of the species. Thus, in the plan of things, when the hatches occur it's like ringing the dinner bell. Food is suddenly available in large quantities and the life of the river is drawn to it like a magnet.

You can sit on the bank and watch it happen. The first insect drifts through and within moments fish will start moving on-station. You can watch individual bugs drift down and you can see the trout come up and take them. Sometimes you can actually see the bugs push through the surface film and emerge. As the hatch progresses, not only are the fish attracted, but birds and other wildlife are as well. The swallows will be on the water, diving low and skimming the surface. The song birds fly out from the bushes.

With the huge variety of insects, the hatches come in many forms. They occur at specific times and they may last an hour or they may last all day. A major hatch will be like a snow storm of insects. The feeding is so aggressive you can stare in amazement at how many fish and bugs there are. Sometimes the insects' behavior is masked and hidden and more difficult to detect. You may have to squint your eye right at the surface of the river to see what's going on. Then there is a special pride in having detected the hatch, in having come that much closer to understanding the rhythm and cycle of the river.

Each hatch is unique, but within the hatches is the struggle of life, death and rebirth. It's a small drama played out again and again and again. It's endlessly fascinating to watch the players play their roles. It is a moment suspended in time. (See the hatch chart in the appendix.)

ANGLING ENTOMOLOGY

When I moved to Camp Sherman, the concept of angling entomology was just coming into vogue. It was the new, hot buzz-word in the fly fishing community. Writers like Ernest Schwiebert were producing fishing books filled with Latin names of insects and suggesting (at least by implication) if you didn't know Latin you couldn't catch fish.

I bought in hook, line and sinker. When I arrived on my new home river, the Metolius, I decided the first order of business would be to catalogue all the hatches. I was going to teach myself entomology by learning the Latin names of each and every insect on the river. I was going to have my own unique, locally adapted fly patterns, too.

In retrospect, I probably couldn't have picked a more difficult challenge. There are not many streams in North America as rich and as diverse as the Metolius. Several nationally known entomology researchers have done work here. All of them consider the river to be an absolute treasure-trove of unique and interesting species.

Herein lies the problem. The scientists' interests and ours, as fishermen and casual observers, are poles apart. They want to find every rare and un-named or unidentified species they possibly can. We want to seek the most common insects and to know which hatch is going to have the most impact on the fish.

This is compounded by the idea that trying to identify insects is not quite like trying to name birds or plants or trees or things like that. All aquatic insects have at least two life stages, many have more. The nymph form is very different from the winged adult, so just trying to connect the two is a challenge. There are look-alike species and wide color variations as well. There's so much complexity that the process of trying to identify an insect by scientific methods becomes a daunting task. It involves microscopic examination and complex scientific keys. At times it becomes downright comical. Species identification of winged adults is often done by examining the male genitalia. (A virgin male, please, we don't want any damaged parts.) You can't help but laugh when you find yourself looking at page after page of drawings of bug penises in an effort to make a positive identification. That's more than most of us ever want to get involved.

I never came close to getting my little cataloguing project done. Over the years I have grown quite un-scientific. I'm willing to make up names when I don't know and I'm the first to admit there are great gaps in my knowledge. After having gone the long way around I have come to the conclusion that, in a practical sense, angling entomology (trying to name things in Latin) is something of a strange off-shoot of fly fishing itself. Far too many angling writers have made a living selling needlessly complicated theories and ideas when the nuts and bolts are quite simple. All you have to do is scoop an insect out of the air. If you have a specimen in hand and you can see its size, shape and color, regardless of whether or not you know its name or its life cycle or anything else about it, you can select a fly to match the hatch. If you see a fish rise, you have a good chance of catching him.

Still, I am not willing to give up the subject of aquatic entomology entirely. For one thing, it's interesting. I like knowing about the bugs in much the same way I like knowing about the birds and plants along the river. After starting to use a screen to collect samples I began to have an appreciation for how rich and diverse the aquatic insect community actually is. I marveled at all the unique and wonderful adaptations these little creatures have found in order to carve out a niche for themselves in this vast, cruel world of ours. If I hadn't gone sampling, I never would have discovered things like the net-spinning caddis with their little, spider web retreats cemented to the rocks, or the swift water mayflies with their flattened bodies clinging so tight that when you bring them up into the air the surface tension allows the water to flow right over them. That's cool stuff – at least it is to me.

In the end, entomology has made me a better observer. It has taught me what to look for and has helped me understand some of the things I am seeing. Many forms of insect behavior are subtle. If you didn't have some kind of advanced knowledge, some hints as to what you're looking at, you could spend a lifetime watching and never realize what you had seen. Mayfly spinners and caddis pupae are elusive little things. Knowing and understanding something about them can only enhance your day.

A LITTLE SUNSHINE

You are well advised to pick and choose your days for winter fishing. The Metolius is close enough to the mountains to make the weather variable. Some years, people cross-country ski by the river, other years there's not much snow at all. But even when there is snow on the bank there can still be good fishing. The rain shadow of the Cascades often causes a break in the storm clouds. A little spot of sunshine will form over the river in the afternoon. That's when you want to fish.

Unless there is some solar input, there's not likely to be much of a hatch. In a cold, even-temperature steam, there is little to start the nymphs stirring without some sunshine. This effect can be so pronounced I have actually seen partly cloudy days when the sun strikes the water and the hatch begins, then a cloud comes over and the hatch dies down again. This cycle can repeat all afternoon. The fisherman casts in the sun and then simply holds fire while the clouds pass. All of the action is dictated by the warmth of the sun.

The tiny mayflies of winter don't hatch in great numbers. When they come (if they come) they look like miniature sailboats as they float down on the current. The feeding activity is usually pretty sporadic. The water is still cold enough that it's not efficient for trout to hold in faster water and pick off their dinner. The calories required for a fish to capture a food item must allow for a net gain. A little, tiny mayfly, which can only have a gazillionth of a calorie of food energy in it, is not a very hearty meal, so it must be taken very quietly and with minimum effort.

Only efficient feeding sites will be active. You have to look for the right place and your time is limited. The hatch never lasts very long. The sun is still low on the horizon and it only peaks up over the crown of the forest for a brief period. By mid-afternoon, shadows will start to form and the river will begin cooling once again. There is only a brief period of good fishing. Still, casting dry flies in February is a pleasant break from a long winter of cabin fever.

4
Caddis in March & April

CADDIS BEHAVIOR

S pring comes slowly to the Metolius. In March and April a rim of green starts to form along the river, but the uplands remain fairly brown and barren. Though it can be warm and pleasant, at times there are still plenty of days when it's dark and cold. We can get snow clear into early May.

These late storms are seldom big ones, just an overnight dusting, a "grass-greener" that brings cool moisture to the budding plants along the river. By noon the snow has melted from the valley floor and there is only a white crown, high on the ridge, to serve as a subtle reminder that winter is not quite ready to relinquish its hold.

The fishing seems to reflect this mood. Despite a succession of caddis hatches and rapidly increasing numbers of insects, there is not much consistent feeding activity yet. You have to search a bit for the opportunity to catch fish. This search is compounded by the fact that caddis hatches can be very difficult to interpret. Mayflies are fairly easy to detect. The insects rest on the water, strengthening their wings before they fly. They'll often drift long distances, inviting the fish to make a rise. This means that cause and effect are visible to the angler. You see the bugs and you see them being taken by the fish.

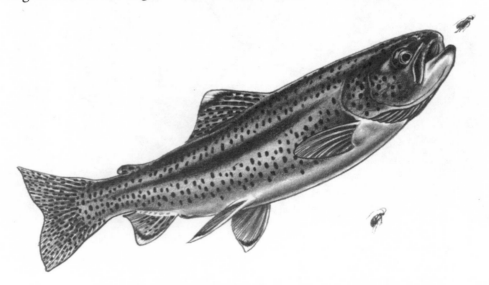

Caddis activity is different. Caddis are of the order Trichoptera or hair-winged insects. Under microscopic examination, their wings are covered with little hair-like structures called setae. The setae allow the insect to trap gasses along the wing, thus at the moment the insect bursts through the river's surface, the wings are dry and ready for flight. The caddis waste no time; you will rarely see them drifting helplessly on the current like mayflies. Once in the air they are very quick and agile fliers that usually leave the river almost immediately. As a result, it's possible to have a very good hatch going on with few bugs visible over the water.

Conversely, there are times when there will be hundreds of caddis moving up-river in migratory flights without causing any reaction from the fish whatsoever. During their life as larvae the caddis often drift downstream. When they emerge as winged adults they have an instinct, built-in, to compensate. They fly up-river right along the banks, retracing their steps. This insures the entire stream will be populated with insects rather than having them all wind up down at the mouth of the river.

When they are engaged in these upstream flights the caddis don't get on the water at all; they're simply not available to the fish. This makes everything very confusing. It's hard to figure out which bugs are hatching and which bugs are flying. There's no correlation between the number of insects you see in the air and the actual hatch activity. This is further compounded by the fact that caddis have a swimming nymph form called a pupa.

CADDIS PUPA

The caddis pupa is an elusive little piece of river life. It is an interim form of development that allows these insects to swim from the bottom of the river to the top. Caddis are what they call a three-stage insect. They appear first as a larva, then as a pupa and finally as a winged adult.

Most of the insect's life, a year or more, is spent as a larva. These worm or grub-like creatures crawl over the river bottom in search of a wide variety of foods. They are generally well protected from the trout because they make a portable shelter out of sand, gravel or woody material like pine needles and bark chips.

When the larva is mature, it seals its case and, much like a caterpillar turning into a butterfly, it transforms into a caddis pupa. Once developed, the pupa will chew out of its case and swim toward the surface. This swimming pupa stage may last only a few minutes before the insect transforms into a winged adult. It is at this point, however, that the insect is the most vulnerable to marauding trout. Unlike the cased larva or the high flying adult, the pupa's only defense is its ability to swim. When it lets go of the bottom and swims upward, it is in the open and clearly visible to the trout.

Unfortunately, these pupae are hidden from us. The life form is so transitory we almost never see it. In a lifetime of fishing I don't think I have seen an actual pupa swimming in the water more than once or twice. There are really only two ways you're likely to obtain a sample. One is from the stomach of a fish (use a sampler rather than killing the fish, please). The other is by opening up a caddis case just before the pupa is ready to hatch. Neither of these sample forms is a living, swimming, kicking, breathing caddis pupa so while they give a model for the general appearance of the pupa, they don't really allow a full appreciation of the living insect and its behavior.

DISTINGUISHING THE HATCH

When I am trying to detect a caddis hatch, I'm forced to watch for clues. I have to use my imagination to visualize the pupae releasing from their cases and then swimming swiftly upward. At the same time, I think about how the trout react by chasing after them. With these thoughts in mind, the first indicator of a hatch is flashes under water. When the trout are chasing pupa they dart and move quite quickly. Sometimes you'll see the flashes of their bodies as they turn. When I see this behavior it's an indicator there is something that the fish are chasing deep underwater. If there are caddis around, it's a good bet that's what the food item is.

A second indicator is an occasional sharp, splashy rise at the surface. The pupae are coming up fast and the fish are chasing them; occasionally the fish will follow all the way to the top. This will result in fairly showy surface rises but, because so much of the activity is still going on underwater, these rises are not consistent, as during a mayfly hatch. You'll hear a splash and then wait several minutes before you hear or see another one. Even though that may not seem like much surface activity, it does indicate a time when fish are likely to be keyed on caddis.

I get my third indicator of a hatch by watching the adult caddis very closely as they dart right over the river's surface. Sometimes you'll see them tumbling on the water for a split second just before they fly away. This odd behavior actually occurs when the insects emerge. Though caddis leave the water quickly, they don't fly instantly. There's usually a momentary pause right at the surface. During this time caddis often make a couple of flaps of their wings before they get airborne, which gives them an appearance of tumbling. When you see this behavior, you can guess there is a hatch going on.

THE INSECTS

The first to arrive, in an ongoing series of spring hatches, is the striped winged caddis or snow sedge. These straw-colored insects are fairly large and easily identified by the distinct horizontal stripe along their wing, clearly visible when they are at rest. You can see the larvae in shallow backwaters along the edge of the river. They are sometimes scattered over the sand by the hundreds. They build a tube-type case out of sand and gravel and often attach pine needles on the side for balance and concealment.

This insect species doesn't seem to have a very good internal clock. Its hatches are more temperature-dependent, rather than being based on a specific time of year. Any time there is a series of warm days, there will be a bit of emerging. The cycle is spread over a long period of time, with the earliest arrivals being seen running along the snow banks in mid-winter, while the later arrivals hatch in March or even early April.

Following the striped wing comes the spring October caddis. That's right, October caddis in March and April. These big orange insects appear on the Metolius both at the beginning and the end of the season. Entomologists tell me this double hatching is not entirely unheard of, but it is rather unusual, just another of the many mysteries of the Metolius. While the fall hatch is larger and more consistent, the April Octobers still bring some pretty good nymph fishing. Large orange caddis pupa imitations, often called carrot nymphs, can be productive. (There are some bull trout fisherman who think this is one of the hottest nymphing periods all season.)

A little later, the smaller caddis begin to appear. The first of two major species you are likely to encounter is what I call the speckled wing caddis or grannom. These insects have a light, mottled brownish-gray wing and a body that is light brown or brownish-olive. On occasion, freshly hatched specimens will show a distinctly light colored side stripe on the body underneath the wing.

The larva of the speckled wing builds a square paper tube case. Sometimes the rocks in the riffles are covered with rows of these shelters. They're all lined up right at the crest of the rock so that the larvae can reach up with their little claw-like front legs and gather whatever food and algae is drifting in the current.

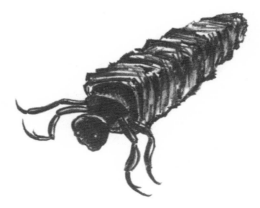

A few weeks behind the speckled wing caddis is a slightly larger light orange or brownish-orange caddis I call the spring sedge. This is a very prolific hatch and these insects engage in some of the most spectacular upstream flights of any of the caddis. Hundreds of insects cruise right along the stream banks, just a few feet off the water, moving upstream like salmon returning from the sea.

This insect is probably a net-spinning caddis of some sort. The large, bright green larvae build a complex spider web-like shelter. Little bits of gravel are incorporated in the web for concealment. For a long time, I didn't appreciate how delicate and beautiful these nets really were. I would find them by picking a rock out of the river, but as soon the sample was out of the water the net would collapse. I thought these shelters were nothing more than a mass of goop on the rock with a little green worm on the inside. One day I happened to examine a shelter under water. When it's submerged and placed in a current, the net floats out and expands. It makes a tube-shaped funnel out of a delicate webbing much like a spider web. The larva has a little hotel at the back, a kind of antechamber where he hides in waiting. When food is caught in the web he comes out to get it. Pretty sophisticated development for nothing more than a little green rockworm.

5
The Hatchery Era

APPLES AND ORANGES

For many years, the Metolius had two kinds of rainbow trout, hatchery and wild. It all started in the 1940's when the river system was not able to sustain a very good harvest. Many factors, no doubt, contributed to this. It's a steep gradient river with limited habitat so it was never able to hold a large population of fish. Then, in the 1920's and 30's, the river started to become a popular vacation spot.

In those early days, harvest was high; people often fed their families on the fish they caught. Old photos from that era show the catches. They'd hang the trout on a rope between two trees or spread them out on a tarp arranged according to size and species. They had some really good fishing back then – incredible numbers of huge trout – but the heyday didn't last long. The Metolius is a fragile ecosystem and it couldn't stand up to that kind of pressure. Soon there were complaints of deteriorating fishing and, in the early 1940's, the Wizard Falls hatchery was built.

The idea seemed good at the time. Give nature a boost. If the river was low on trout, just add more. It was like planting more wheat in the fields but, sadly, it didn't work out quite as planned. Early managers didn't fully appreciate how complex fish populations can be, nor did they understand the value of genetically adapted fish in their own native habitat. For them all rainbow trout were roughly alike, the more the merrier.

The hatchery fish were an inferior product. Pen-reared in captivity, they were not able to adapt in a natural environment. I think my daughter, Michelle, told the story best. When she was a small girl, probably three or four years old, we used to go fishing together. I would hook the trout and she would land them. For some reason she studied this fish a lot harder than usual. Finally she looked up to me, puzzled, and asked, "Daddy, why is it sick?" For a moment, I didn't understand what she was talking about. It looked like a perfectly normal rainbow trout to me. Then suddenly I realized what she was seeing. It was a hatchery fish, apparently she'd never seen one before.

In those days it was possible to be selective with your method, you could choose whether to catch hatchery fish or wild. If your approach was to imitate natural foods with a dead drift presentation, you would catch mostly natives.

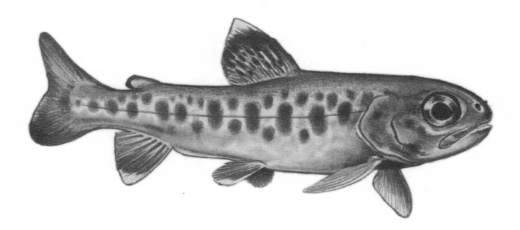

The stockers, on the other hand, didn't seem to know what natural foods were, so you caught them with flies that looked like the pellets from the hatchery or by doing things that made your fly stand apart. Stripping and twitching the flies underwater was extremely popular.

When we caught this fish, my daughter recognized immediately that it was different. She saw that it didn't have the normal rainbow colors or the natural camouflage. It was matched to the concrete tank where it had been raised; it clearly didn't belong. To her it looked sick.

Sometimes, out of the mouths of babes we hear the greatest truth. There are many who would have argued her assessment, and many who thought that hatchery stocking was the best thing that ever happened to the Metolius, but this little girl told honestly what she saw. The hatchery fish were not fit, they were not able to adapt to the stream, they were not an acceptable substitute. They were as different from the natives as apples are to oranges.

The Research

In the first few years of stocking, managers attempted to use a put-and-grow approach. They stocked small, fingerling-sized trout hoping they would naturally adapt. The results were not good. The program very quickly moved over to stocking catchable, legal-sized rainbow trout. There was no longer any thought of naturalizing, the goal was simply to augment harvest.

This put-and-take program became quite popular. In a way, it was a self-fulfilling prophecy. It set up what the biologists call adverse spatial interaction. What happens is, the more you stock, the more you reduce the standing crop of native fish. Since hatchery fish don't survive well in the wild, the more you reduce the native fish, the more you become dependent on stocking. The day the first truckload of fish was put into the river, a vicious cycle was set in motion.

A landmark study done in Montana, called the Vincent study, explains how all this interaction works. In essence, each river has a fixed holding capacity dictated by the available habitat. Fish need specific things to survive: food, shelter from current, and protection from predators. There are only so many places in a river where a fish can find these elements. Theoretically, if you could count the number of niches where a fish can live you would come up with a figure that represents the stream's holding capacity. Obviously, in real life it's a little more complicated than that, but the basic idea is sound.

When hatchery fish of catchable size are stocked in large numbers, as they were on the Metolius, the available habitat becomes flooded. Many smaller native fish are displaced, pushed out into marginal or unsurvivable habitats. The overall standing crop of wild fish is reduced. Unfortunately, the hatchery fish that have displaced these natives are only temporary residents. Because of their lack of adaptation, research shows that the survival of legal-size trout stocked into a natural river environment is almost zero. The natives are gone and soon the hatchery fish are gone as well. In the end, the stocking that was meant to boost fish populations actually causes them to decline. A "boom-or-bust" cycle is set in motion. Fishermen experience very high highs and low lows. Right after stocking, the habitat is flooded. Everybody is catching fish. Very soon it

drops into the down cycle. There are great expanses of empty, fishless river and anglers are calling for another load of fish from the hatchery.

By the mid-70's, this cycle had become fully entrenched on the Metolius. It was so noticeable you could actually see the decline in fishing success through the week. They would stock on Friday for the weekend, by Monday, fishing was going downhill. On Wednesday and Thursday, folks were begging for the truck to come around again. The villain had become the hero. Despite the fact that Fish and Wildlife statistics showed angler success rates going steadily downhill throughout the sixty years of stocking, people still believed that the hatchery was the answer and that more stocked trout was the only way to improve the river. Eventually, it became so skewed that one biologist actually told me there were no significant populations of native trout in the Metolius and that there probably never had been any. It was widely believed that, without the hatchery, there would be no fishing.

CODE OF CONDUCT

In our house, when I was a boy growing up, fishing always had a special meaning. It was almost like there was a spiritual overtone. The outdoor experience was set apart and sanctified, there were rules and a code of conduct. My father always taught me, "Never kill more fish than you can use and never overfish a stream. The river is the source of our sport." he told me sternly, "Never do anything that will harm it."

In those days, we looked on all forms of stocking as a benefit. We may have been naïve, but it fit into our thinking because in both the east and the Rocky Mountain west, where I learned to fish, most of the native species were long gone. The trout we caught had all been introduced. I remember my Dad talking about it once. We were high on a bridge overlooking a stream somewhere in Connecticut. We could look down into the pool and see a pod of

freshly stocked trout. Dad didn't try to catch them, instead he threw rocks into the pool, trying to scatter the fish. "We want those trout to spread out," he told me. "We want them to replenish the river so we can have better fishing later."

As I began to understand more clearly how stocking really worked, as I lost my rose-colored glasses, I found myself increasingly offended. The program on the Metolius was not intended to replenish the stream. Managers knew that 90% of the trout caught would be taken within the first five days after stocking. They were acting strictly to promote harvest. This idea seemed almost childish to me. What kind of an ego does a sportsman have if he is supposedly engaged in an outdoor activity and yet he needs to catch fish so badly he wants somebody to hide trout under every rock? That's like a child wanting the tooth fairy to put money under the pillow. It made no sense to me.

The fact that this put-and-take fishery came at the expense of the real residents of the river made me mad. As this anger grew, I was faced with some choices. The first one was easy. Catch and release fly fishing was starting to come into vogue and I liked the idea. Even though the few fish I was putting back represented a small contribution, I vowed not to kill any more trout out of the Metolius. It made me feel good to know I was doing the right thing. But just limiting my own harvest didn't feel like enough. I wanted to encourage others to do the same, so I began to speak out. I started writing articles about catch and release and wild fish in the newspaper and I joined with other fishermen. A fledgling movement to promote native fish on the Metolius began to form.

THE FIN-CLIPPED RULE

The fish wars lasted for almost 20 years. It took a long time to get from the first proposals to a wild trout stream. There were a lot of meetings, a lot of studies, a lot of arguments, and more than enough hard feelings to go around. Hundreds, perhaps even thousands, of people became involved. Amongst the first were the Santiam Fly Casters from Salem, Oregon. Right in the beginning they passed a club resolution to promote wild fish management on the Metolius. Little did they know what they were getting into.

Before it was over, most of the organized fly fishing clubs in the region had become involved. In the end, the battle had statewide implications. The leading wild fish advocacy group in the Northwest, Oregon Trout, can trace its roots directly to the Metolius conflict.

The first proposal in support of native fish was made by the Santiam group. They wanted to try a small wild trout test area somewhere on the river. Instead, the Department of Fish and Wildlife offered a compromise; they agreed to mark all the hatchery fish with an adipose fin clip. All the wild fish were given protection, they had to be released unharmed.

When this rule was first put into effect, those of us on the wild fish side didn't like it all that well. The stocked trout were still there, depressing the native fish population. It was only a partial solution, one that didn't address the issue of interaction. We thought it missed the point rather badly. In retrospect, it turned out to be a very good rule, probably the best thing to happen throughout the fish wars. For the first time, a separate value was placed on wild fish. People who had never thought about it before began to realize there was a distinction. It wasn't long before it was a badge of honor to catch a native. When you hooked a fish, people would immediately ask, "Is it wild?" An important awareness started to grow.

BATTLE LINES

The awareness grew slowly, though. There were still plenty of fishermen who didn't like the idea of catch and release at all. For them, the harvest was an important part of the whole fishing ritual. They took it to be a personal right. They were determined to see the stocking program continue, and so the battle lines were drawn. Some of the strongest supporters of the hatchery program were business owners. Even though most of them didn't fish, they spoke with a loud and unified voice. They didn't want that tourist apple cart to be upset.

Many of us in the wild fish community spent time researching and trying to explain. We didn't think Camp Sherman was going to turn into a barren desert and that everybody would leave just because you couldn't keep fish anymore, so we gathered information about what had happened in other areas where stocking was discontinued. The results were always the same. The resident, stream-spawned fish flourished and businesses profited and grew. Good fishing is, after all, the key. But this didn't matter, our words of explanation fell on deaf ears.

As the fight heated up, sentiments grew so strong there were people who didn't want to talk to me anymore. I became a focal point because of my writing and my outspoken opinions. One business owner even tried to run me down with a pick-up truck. This was not an attempted assassination on the highway, it was more like a low-speed assault in the parking lot. Still, he swerved at me and I had to jump out of the way. I would have been injured if I hadn't been quick on my feet.

Perhaps the saddest encounter was with the former owner of the Camp Sherman store. Mind you, this man no longer runs the store, and his actions should not reflect on the current store owners: they're much nicer people. This man was a well-known curmudgeon. On this particular day, my daughter and I had been down to the river, fishing. On the way back, she gathered a bouquet of violets. Before we went home, we stopped at the store for an ice cream. I was sitting on the porch-step, leaning against the post, enjoying my treat while my daughter was out in the parking lot, playing. She left her violets on the step beside me. When the store owner came up he looked at the violets, then looked at me, then, very deliberately, he stepped on the wild flowers and ground them into the deck. I was left to try to explain to my daughter why the mean man had destroyed her pretty bouquet.

CASUALTIES OF WAR

There is only one regret from the fish wars, and that's some of the friends we lost. A few of the older fishermen had become dependent on the hatchery trout and they got hurt when things began to change. Stocked fish are an illusion, of a sort. They look like part of the stream even though they're not. Before the conflict, nobody made any distinctions. Most people wore wicker creels, and anything that got caught was killed and put in them.

After the fin-clipped rule came into effect, people had to start thinking a little bit more and a few fellows were caught on the wrong side. Harold Beach was one of them. Harold was a fine gentleman and a fly fisherman through and through. Over the course of many years on the Metolius he developed a complex fishing system with intricate strips and twitches. He kept meticulous records on all the fish he caught: how he caught them, when, and where. Afterwards he would graph all this information out on his computer. He had years of data.

Unfortunately, Harold never bothered to ask one big question. He never looked at the origin of the fish he was catching. He treated them all alike. As it turned out, his whole fishing system was designed to catch hatchery trout. When this was revealed, I think it hurt Harold deeply. I asked him about it once and he told me he was too old to change. When the stocking ended, Harold quit fishing altogether. That broke my heart. I wished I could have found a way to help him transition. The river was not the same without him.

Still, I could not change and go back. Everything that was done to benefit the wild trout has had a positive impact. When the pressure of stocking was finally lifted in 1996, the wild fish population bloomed. Spawning ground counts went up and so did angler success. Today, there's hardly anyone left who would like to go back to the old way. The new generation of business owners is wild fish conscious, they recognize what a rare and valuable resource we have. The Metolius has become a poster child for native fish and a shining example of what enlightened management can do. People today are catching more and bigger fish than they have in years. The river has made a dramatic comeback. It's starting to be like it was in the good old days; in the good old days before the hatchery.

6
Early May

SPRING WARMTH

During March and April, the signs of spring come slowly, almost grudgingly, to the river. This changes dramatically in May, when the season comes rushing in with all its glory. The weather takes on a summery feel, people begin to wear tee-shirts and shorts. Some of the girls start wearing halter tops and the wild flowers begin to bloom. Right below the bridge in Camp Sherman there's a large Snowberry bush. Like clockwork, it flowers on Mother's Day —

the second Sunday in May.

When the weather turns warm, keep your eye out for the carpenter ants. The forest around the Metolius is full of them and any rotting stump will be riddled with their burrows. On the first really hot, sunny day, the whole population will start moving. For a brief period they will be flying and crawling everywhere. The triggering mechanism is air temperature. Without a thermometer, you'll know it has slipped over the 80°F mark. Summer's coming!

As the sun angle climbs higher, the light penetrates deeper and deeper into the river. The water's color changes from dark and somber to a beautiful blue/green. It's an almost iridescent color in the deep pools, below the rapids, where extra oxygen has been pounded into the water. As the river basks in the sunshine, there are small daily spikes in the water temperature when the cold spring water is heated by the sunshine. The warmer river temperatures activate the cold-blooded fish and insects. Hatches become more abundant, the fish feed more freely, and the river becomes more friendly and inviting.

The Small Mayflies

From mid-April on, anglers start looking for the first of the green drakes. This is the most popular hatch of the year and it is eagerly anticipated. Some anglers try to jump the gun, but in the beginning the hatch is not very consistent and it is hard to predict. One day you'll see some drakes, the next day you won't. If you're lucky, you may get a few bonus fish but it's not something you should plan on.

The smaller mayflies create better, more consistent fishing. The lead insect in this hatch is the gray/olive baetis mayfly. It's one of the most common insects on the river. It has multiple brood cycles, meaning there may be as many as four or five generations in a single season hatching all year long. It's a rare day that you don't see at least a few them on the water in the early afternoon. At certain times, the hatch pulses up and thickens and it can become quite prolific. Early May is as good a spike as any.

When the baetis flourish, it's common to have a second species of yellow/olive mayfly join in. This is what's called a mixed hatch with two insects emerging at the same time. These yellowish insects are not multi-brooded like the baetis, they're actually a series of hatches of a variety of different insects. While they can be distinguished in hand, the effort hardly seems worth it. I've always lumped them together and treated them as one.

During these hatches, the gray baetis generally out-number the yellow/olives by quite a bit, but that doesn't mean they always create the majority of the feeding activity. Sometimes the fish will be focused on the gray mayfly, sometimes the yellow; individual fish will have personal preferences. You can catch three fish in a row on the gray then you'll run onto one that won't eat until you show it yellow. It can be frustrating and you have to be careful not to spend your whole day switching back and forth from one pattern to the other.

MASKING HATCHES

Sometimes, there can be odd mayflies mixed in with the standard grays and yellows. It's a test of your powers of observation. All through the spring there are powerful bursts of hatch activity from a variety of un-named species. The hatch duration is usually very short, often less than a week, so these are not hatches you plan on, they are events you encounter.

One of the most common of these is the miniature green drake. I recall the first time I ran into it. There was a flush hatch of the regular gray and yellow mayflies going on. Fish were feeding steadily, but I spent most of my time changing flies. I just couldn't get it right and kept going back and forth. The fish's half-hearted rolls told me I was close, but the missed strikes told me the magic ingredient was still not there. Finally, I sat down on a rock to observe. I figured it was better to try to learn something than to flog the water any longer. I concentrated on an area where a large fish had been feeding actively and studied the surface of the river intently. I wanted to see if I could actually pick out which of the insects this fish was eating.

I quickly saw there was a third mayfly in the mix which I had not seen before. I think I missed it because it was not as prevalent as either of the other two species. I watched one of the mystery insects drift into range – slurp – it was gone. The yellow and gray mayflies drifted through by the dozens. Nothing happened. Another mystery bug; it was taken, too. In the midst of this absolutely flush hatch of common insects, there was some sort of oddball species on which the fish were keying.

I shifted my research to a nearby eddy where I wanted to capture a sample. Soon, my specimen came drifting by and I netted it with my hat. It looked like a miniature version of a green drake. It had relatively tall, slate gray wings, the thorax was dark green, the abdomen had distinct dark and light green segmented bands. Later, at home, I searched through my books. The insect appeared to be a member of the Flavilina family of mayflies. The writers called them Flavs for short. These miniature green drakes are fairly common throughout the Northwest. Over the years it has become a favorite hatch because my first experience demonstrated, Flavs have a lot of horsepower to draw fish up to a rise.

The lesson to be drawn from a hatch like this is that nothing is cast in stone. No matter how well you think you know the hatch, there can be day-to-day fluctuations. Many anglers don't like the Metolius because they think it's too hard. I agree it can be difficult – it's a river that will test you – but that's what I like. After a lifetime of fishing, I'm still discovering new things all the time and I'm sure I'll never exhaust the options; it will never become routine. Your skill will always be tested and you will be measured by your ability to adapt.

GRAY DAYS

The sunshine in May is the thing that drives the river's engine. Everyone loves it. After a long, protracted, cold spring it is delightful to strip down to a tee-shirt and let the sunshine bake your skin. Still, as much as I revel in the sunny days, it's the gray, overcast ones that really make for great fishing.

The dominant hatches of spring are mostly mayflies. In his book, *The Mayfly, The Angler, and the Trout*, Fred Arbona explains why these insects are anti-phototropic – why they don't like bright sunlight. It's based on their life cycle. The mayflies hatch as duns, these duns emerge from the water and fly to the bushes. Within twenty-four hours, they will shed their outer skin and change from duns to clear-winged spinners. After that, they return to the river, mate, and die. In order to shed from a dun to a spinner, the mayfly must keep it's outer skin soft and supple. If the insect is exposed to too much sun, the skin becomes dry and brittle and the spinner will be trapped inside the husk, unable to emerge and complete its cycle.

In order to promote a more successful transition, nature has equipped mayflies with the ability to wait for preferred light conditions. Once the nymphs are ripe, they can hold off for as much as a week, looking for a low-light day on which to hatch. From a fisherman's perspective, this means that the perfect time to be on the river is a cloudy, wet day right after a solid week of sunshine. All the insects that have been holding off will hatch in a single afternoon.

When it starts to rain, many fishermen will call it quits. They'll hang around the house grumpy and unhappy because the weather has turned sour. While they're cussing, I've canceled appointments and rearranged my schedule so I can go fishing. I can hardly wait to get to the water. On the river there's a special mood. Geese are nesting and the green of the riverbanks is absolutely brilliant; the new young plants are bursting with vitality after the soaking they've just received. The heaviness of the clouds hanging over the top ridge has a powerful, even slightly eerie feeling. On the path down to the river, raindrops make little silver sparkles on the tips of the pine needles. Even before I get to the water I'm fidgeting, just waiting for the first mayflies to appear. The trout are going to feed. I'm going to see the Metolius in all her glory. For a dry fly fisherman, it doesn't get any better.

7
Wood and Wildflowers

WIND IN THE PINES

On a spring day, when the flowers bloom, it is difficult to reflect back on the hardships of winter past. But winter, wood and wildflowers are all tied together as one. On a cold night in January, the storm winds sweep down from the mountains and into the valley with a mighty force. From a high vantage point, these gusts seem to ripple through the pines like a gentle breeze through a field of summer wheat. But these are not simple blades of grass, these are 150 foot pines, four feet at the butt, bowing to the fury of nature.

The roar of these mighty gusts travels far down the wind. At first, it sounds like the churning of a river heard from a distance. It's a steady background noise that gradually grows. The wind is racing over the canopy at thirty or forty miles an hour, and still each gust takes several minutes to arrive. For a moment, while you wait, it's strangely quiet down on the forest floor, then the gusts sweep over. Limbs crack and the trees bend and twist, contorting violently in ways you would not imagine giant pines could move. Out in the distance, there are things falling. In that moment, coming to see the storm doesn't seem like such a good idea anymore.

Next morning, there are limbs and pine needles scattered all over the road. In one spot a tree has blown down. There are shingles off a roof and a fence is leaning. Down on the river there will be changes, too. At the end of winter, after the snow is gone, I will start to venture out to the more remote parts of the river once again.

When I have been away for a while, it's like coming back to see an old friend, only my friend has changed a bit. He's gained a little weight, or lost some hair, or become a little more gray. It takes a while to get used to him again. In the same way the river has changed. Perhaps a logjam has been swept out and a favorite fishing hole is filled in with sand. At another spot, a tree has fallen in fast water, causing a current break and a new place for fish. Blown down trees and limbs have collected everywhere.

When that first day of exploring is over, I have cast my fly very little. I'm too busy poking and prodding and looking at the fine detail of the little changes that nature has made. In the words of the late Charles Brooks, it truly is, A Living River.

WOOD AS HABITAT

Studies by Forest Service research biologist Jim Sidell have shown that large woody matter in streams affects almost every aspect of river life, from insect, to fish, to the very shape of the river itself. Early explorers, Lewis and Clark among them, often commented about the timber-choked rivers and streams they encountered as they traveled in the Northwest. Waterways were described as being thatched with downed trees and logs, at times nearly impenetrable.

The Metolius was no exception. Newspaper reports from 1938, documenting the first attempt to float the river by boat, said it took four days to get through to the town of Warm Springs on the Deschutes. Over 20 portages were made in order to get around all the fallen timber. There were massive logjams spanning the entire river. Today, a boat can pass through much of the same area in a matter of hours. At worst, you will encounter occasional spanning logs.

There are no major jams anymore. You have to go up to the smaller tributaries, places like the head of Jack Creek, Upper Canyon Creek or Candle and Jefferson Creeks, to see what the stream must have looked like at the turn of the century.

This begs the question, what happened to all the timber? A stream survey in 1942 reports that the first clearing of the river was done by a logging company, in preparation for a timber drive. They blasted out all the rocks and snags. The drive was abandoned after a test run (which, I'll venture to say, was a wild ride for the loggers). Since that time, removal of wood for scenic purposes and rafting safety has kept the river relatively free of blockages. It's only in recent years that newer, more enlightened forest management practices have allowed some of the wood to start to collect once again.

This loss of timber has no doubt had many subtle effects on the ecosystem and the health of the river. From a fisherman's perspective, perhaps the biggest problem is loss of habitat for fish. The Metolius is a very steep-gradient stream, averaging a drop of nearly 35 feet per mile. This is more than twice the fall of such famous whitewater streams as the Deschutes, Rogue or even the Colorado in the Grand Canyon. The relatively new volcanic geology of the area has created a steep, straight, rapidly eroding streambed.

Biologically, such a stream is not a very dynamic environment for fish; a greater pool-to-riffle ratio is preferred. Fish need a more diverse habitat, more calm spots, more breaks in the rapids, more twists and bends in the stream to afford proper resting, feeding and spawning areas. Providing this habitat diversity is a critical role for wood in the Metolius.

By extrapolating from the historical data and by examining the oral history, we can guess that before the intervention of the loggers, rafters and homeowners there may have been enough wood to create a full river blockage every couple of miles. Between the major logjams, there would have been other minor obstructions as well. These big log blockades would have created marvelous habitat. The damming effect would have backed up large pools and put twists and bends in the river. In my mind's eye, I can see the fish tucked back in among the snags, darting out to capture green drakes and golden stoneflies.

WOOD AND WILDFLOWERS

Wood in the river also has an important effect on the streambank plant community. When logs fall into the water, they don't remain barren and raw for very long. A debris mat forms quite quickly on the upstream side. In the small eddies at the base of the log, rafts of pine needles, leaves and other forest debris collect. At first these mats are free-floating on the river's surface, but they are fed constantly with more material. Larger limbs may be added, sticks and bark as well. The mat grows until it is several inches thick. In these mats there are seeds and roots and tubers delivered by the river. In the spring they begin to sprout and grow and a little hydroponic garden starts to form along the log. By June, a log that fell in January will have a small plant community forming along it.

Over the next few years, these plant colonies expand rapidly. The roots tend to bind the debris mass together and make it stronger. The original plants die and fall back on the logs. Leaves and pine needles collect. The logs themselves decay and add to the compost. Gradually, a rich humus soil begins to form. Within a span of no more than five of six years, a rather sizable plant community has taken shape.

These colonies are constantly growing, changing shape and adjusting. It's a very dynamic process. I know one spot where a piece of riverbank, with a cluster of half-a-dozen small alder trees on it, became undercut. The piece broke off and somehow managed to float upright for about a quarter of a mile until it fetched up against a log. The whole thing, soil and all, was an instant transplant. The alders took root and grew – they're still there today.

Sometimes the log and plant community will cause a current break, causing sand and silt to collect on the downstream side. At first, water weeds invade, then grasses, and gradually other plants. In this way, a colony can expand its own landmass.

When high-water events occur, the logs shift and move. Surprisingly, they often go with their plant communities intact. Some logs will be pushed flat along the banks while other logs collect into piles. These logs become thatched and interwoven, with plants growing up between them.

There are hundreds, if not thousands, of these log structures up and down the river. Many have become small islands, in all stages of development ranging from new logs, just starting, to older logs that have developed into land masses of several acres or more. Whenever you find a small, watery back channel, even if it is nothing more than a bog area behind an island, a search toward the upstream end will almost certainly reveal a log pile that started it all.

At one spot, below Bridge 99, there's a truly amazing island. This part of the river, near the horn of the Metolius, is a particularly active place for logjams. The river widens and shallows briefly and logs have always collected there. The river channel is braided with a series of small islands. To get to one of my favorite fishing holes, you cross a shallow back channel and then bushwhack across a small, heavily timbered island. For years, I thought this place was a solid landmass. Then one day I discovered an odd hole out in the center of it. I could look eight or ten feet down to the riverbed where there was a trickle of water flowing. When I explored further with my flashlight, I could look underneath the island well back into the caverns below the logs. It was only then that I realized the entire land structure was built on top of an enormous logjam.

Once they fall in the river, logs may last for several hundred years before they decay completely. They'll spend all that time growing and building a plant community around themselves. When you explore carefully, you'll find most of the rich wildflower deposits and the most verdant river growth associated in one way or another with a tree that has fallen in the river. The Metolius is actually converting wood into wild flowers.

THE BLOOM OF SPRING

When the flowers bloom in May, June and July it is a sight to behold. As far as you can see in either direction, up and down the river corridor, the banks are covered with white blooms hung on a spring-green drape. The nine-bark bushes and the snowberries are in bloom. Below them, in the foreground, interwoven into the logjams, are the white, plate-sized heads of the cow parsnips. Underneath them are the two-foot flower stalks of blue river lupines just coming into bloom. For accent, right at the water's edge, the snapdragon-like monkey flowers and a dozen other species are draped all around.

In the forest, under the trees, the smaller upland lupines are spread in a carpet, the bitter brush is in bloom and there are wild roses, too. In some places you will find mountain lilies, tiger lilies and lady slippers. In the wet spots there are bog orchids and elephant heads, and giant skunk cabbage with leaves the size of a small coffee table. It is a wonderful garden.

The sun's heat raises the perfume of the forest into the still air. The smells drift downwind on a gentle, almost imperceptible breeze. One moment you'll be enshrouded in a cloud of rose scent, the next moment it is the sweet perfume of the bitter brush. There are breaths of hot pine interspersed with the cool, moist smell of the river. Sometimes, it so overwhelming you can't trace where all the smells are coming from. You get a whiff of roses, fresh and strong, but when you turn around there are no roses anywhere to be seen even though their smell is drifting through the forest. It is delightfully mysterious, and a wonderful treat to the senses that makes me laugh out loud. To go fishing in spring, you have to wade in the wildflowers before you can wade in the river.

8
Green Drakes

A Green Drake Moment

I was with a friend on a favorite section of the river, following my usual practice of leap-frogging along, fishing the best spots for a bit and then moving. We had tried several nice runs and hadn't seen much happening, but by mid-afternoon our patience paid off. The green drakes began to appear and the trout started to rise, at first sporadically, then more steadily. Everything was working out just right, we were catching fish and laughing it up pretty good and enjoying ourselves immensely.

For our next stop, we moved to a place where there are some swirling eddies tucked under the trees, along the edge of a very deep pool. It is a tough spot to fish, but for someone willing to do the bushwhacking, it can be productive.

My friend and I had crawled down the bank and then ducked in under the brush to a spot where there was a little opening from which we could make some small casts. We were sitting next to the water doing a little leader repair when the vision appeared. A flat spot in the surface currents passed by and we saw three beautiful big rainbows lined up along the edge of the drop-off. It was a perfect picture. We never would have seen them hidden in shade if they had not been backlit against the slanting rays of sunshine piercing down into the deep water of the pool. The fish looked jet black silhouetted against a curtain of swirling blue/green water. All were in the eighteen inch-plus class.

My friend looked at me wide-eyed. I'm sure he had never seen a set-up quite like that before. It was a classic green drake moment, the fish were obviously there to feed. A trout simply would not hold in that kind of current unless it was getting food, and lots of it. Just a flick of the rod would put our flies in front of them. He could hardly speak, "Did you see that?" he stammered.

"Cast a fly," I suggested, motioning toward the water.

THE INSECT

Ephemerella Grandis, the green drake, is one insect I do know by its Latin name. It is without question the premier hatch on the Metolius. No other insect has quite so profound an effect.

The drakes begin to appear, on a consistent basis, in mid to late May. The hatch lasts through June, extending sometimes even into the first or second week of July. These insects are quite beautiful in their own right. They have a gracefully curved body, thin, delicate tails, and tall, upright, slate-gray wings. The thorax is dark green, the abdomen a lighter yellow/olive with very distinct dark green banding. On many specimens there is a splash of yellow right at the base of the wing. If you handle them carefully, the drakes will sit quietly in the palm of your hand and let you admire them from different angles.

The overall length of the insect is more than an inch. It is quite robust too, which makes them one of the largest insects in the mayfly family. Their thick bodies contain significant amounts of protein. The mature insects float helplessly on the river surface for extended periods, drying and strengthening their wings before they take flight. They often stretch with a flapping motion. Flap once and they'll attract a lot of attention. Flap twice and they're converted to fish food.

It's an ideal situation for the trout - a good food source that's easy to capture. Even the largest native rainbows, the ones some people call myth fish, will come out of hiding and up to the surface for these insects. There's no other time when the fish can be seen and caught with such relative ease.

THE HATCH

Fishing a green drake hatch is Tom Sawyer time; it reminds me of barefoot boys with cane poles. This is a lazy, ambling hatch. The wild flowers are in bloom and the weather is perfect. It would be a good time to go fishing even if there was nothing happening at all. The fish keep gentlemen's hours, so there's no need to get on the water early. The bugs don't appear until mid-to late-afternoon. Usually it's sometime between two and four pm before the hatch gets going.

While there are green drakes found all along the river, by far the best concentrations are below the confluence of Jack Creek. At Jack Creek there is a thermocline, or temperature change, which separates the river into two distinct habitats. It's very common to have one set of hatches going on above the demarcation and a second set below.

This temperature variation is created by the springs. The water sources toward the head of the river drain from the area around the Santiam Pass and Mount Washington. They average about 48°F. The next series of springs, around Jack Creek and Canyon Creek, come from up on Three Finger Jack. This series of springs is much colder, with average temperatures close to 40°F. As these colder springs blend with the water from the warmer springs, the river's temperature drops from 48°F to about 44°F. This sets up the thermocline. The best green drake hatches occur on the colder side, downstream from Jack Creek.

I like to be on the water well in advance of the hatch so I can get my waders on, fix my leader, and loosen up my casting arm a bit. In this way, the hatch becomes a waiting game. It leaves plenty of time to sniff wildflowers and watch the river flow. It's a very pleasant time. I wander along the river, flipping my fly halfheartedly, enjoying whatever the day has to bring.

When the hatch starts, I'll usually see a single green drake drifting up-river on the afternoon breeze. The insects fly tail down with a fluttering wing beat. They leave the water slowly, looking like miniature crosses suspended in the air. Within minutes of seeing the first one, both fish and drakes will start to show themselves all along the river. It is time to go to work and the lazy, ambling part is over.

Once the bugs start to hatch, there is a certain sense of urgency. The hatch seldom lasts more than a couple of hours and there are days when there may only be thirty or forty minutes of prime action. In that time I want to be focused and efficient. I don't want to waste time or squander casts. I try to pick out the location of individual fish by their rise and cast directly to them. It may take me several tries to get the fly in the right spot, but very seldom will I get turned down completely. The power of the green drake is such that even the most suspicious fish will usually give me at least the courtesy of a roll and a look at the fly.

Toward the end of the hatch, activity fades slowly as the bugs gradually dissipate. The fish slow down and then finally quit feeding altogether. At this point, the targets of individual trout are gone, so I switch to searching tactics. A fly drifting on a good feeding lane will often trigger a response even after the hatch has been over for a while. It's as if the fish are saying, "One more, just give me one more of those delicious bugs."

When the searching patterns stop working in the main current, there's still one last opportunity. During any hatch, there will be a certain number of crippled and partially emerged insects that failed to make it into the air. They will be swept along to collect in the eddies and backwaters. Fish stay active on this feed well after all the other surface activity is over. Eventually, the eddy fishing dies off, too. The caddis start flying, and the shadows lengthen. The fish are done for the day.

It's always a little disappointing at the end. No matter how many fish I have caught, I could always use one more. I never want to quit and go home. Still, back at the car, when I am stripping off my waders, I feel well satisfied. It's been a good day and I'm content.

NYMPHS AND SPINNERS

Green drake nymphs never seem to attract much interest from fly fishermen. I suppose that's at least in part because the dry fly fishing is so good. Most of us would prefer, if possible, to fish top water. Still, the drake nymph is a sizable food item and it shouldn't be overlooked completely.

These nymphs spend up to two years roaming the river bottom before they hatch. They are in the crawler family of mayflies, a grazer type of insect that lives on plant material, algae and organic debris from the surrounding forests. By maturity they are quite stocky, almost as large as some stoneflies. Their body is covered with little spines almost like a horned toad or a miniature dinosaur. When captured, they have a curious habit of backing into a corner of your hand and arching their tail over their back like a scorpion. They look rather menacing, but they are actually quite harmless – a good mouthful for a trout. I've had success with nymphal imitations both in the early spring just before the insects come to maturity and in the pre-hatch a few hours before the insects emerge.

Another way to squeeze a little extra out of a green drake hatch is to look for the spinner falls. Literature says these green drake spinners return to the river to lay their eggs some time after dark, suggesting they don't offer much of a fishing opportunity. My observations don't bare that out entirely. Late in the hatch, from mid-June into July, I have, on occasion, encountered spinner falls around 8:30 or 9:00 in the morning. While this behavior is not as predictable as the hatch of duns, it can create some excellent fishing.

In the early morning, the river stays in shade for a long time. The early rays of sunlight come in slanting shafts down through the tall trees. When the angle is right, you can see the delicate wings of the spinners glint in the sunlight. The insects are flying in large mating columns, moving up and down rhythmically. As the sun gets closer to the water, so do the insects and actual touchdown occurs simultaneously.

Almost immediately, the eggs are deposited and the females fall flush on the river, spent, their clear wings outstretched. The spinners are actually in the surface film, more than on it and from a distance they are almost impossible to see. If you go to an eddy to collect specimens, the bugs will look like green bumblebees on the water.

As soon as the spinners touch the water, the feeding activity starts. It seems to come out of nowhere and it's pretty intense. If you were unaware of the spinners coming on, it could be a little startling. You would, no doubt, spend some time looking for the right fly. I just use a standard green drake. It can offer a good hour to hour-and-a-half of bonus dry fly fishing.

AN OPPORTUNITY

On the way home from a day of green drake fishing, I like to stop by the old general store in Camp Sherman and get either a pop or a beer, depending on my mood. It's a moment in which I can share my day, trade stories, and find out how others have been doing.

When we're swapping lies like this, I always seem to run across one or two people who are grumbling. They haven't had any success, or at least not enough to content them. I always feel a little sorry for these guys. I'd like everybody to catch fish if possible, but I also have to wonder what's going on. How can it be, in the midst of the best fishing of the year, there are people who are missing it completely? Sometimes the answer is simple. The fishermen just haven't done their homework. They're in the wrong part of the river or fishing the wrong part of the day. These are normal mistakes, easy enough to repair. Learning these kinds of things is part of paying dues; part of becoming a fly fisherman.

Other times, the answer is not so simple. These people are trying to make the river fit their own ideas of how things should be. One guy might want fishing to fit around a tee time and he can't understand why nature won't co-operate. Another fellow may have unrealistic expectations because he has watched a few too many fishing shows or listened to too many braggarts brag. He has come with some idea that he is going to set the fly fishing world on fire.

Unfortunately, it doesn't always work that way. Score keeping on the Metolius is usually a losing proposition because the river doesn't lend itself to big numbers; we already know it's a limited habitat. Physically, there aren't as many niches for fish as other rivers might have. That means, quite simply, that during a short duration hatch like the green drakes, if you count the time it takes to walk from one hole to the next, and the fish you're going to miss, plus all the other little problems like broken leaders and what-not, you're simply not going to get that many chances. If you have a five or six fish day you've done well. Never, ever will you catch fifty fish. The Metolius is just not a big numbers stream.

I look for moments, not for numbers for my contentment. Over the years, I have captured dozens and dozens of these moments in my mind in vivid detail. All I have to do is close my eyes and I'm there, smelling the wild flowers, feeling the sunshine, and watching a beautiful speckled back rainbow turn on my fly. That's where I get my pleasure.

This is a world-class river with some of the most beautiful rainbows you will ever see in a wild, natural environment. If, for a moment, you can get in tune with that enough so that you have the opportunity to see one magnificent fish, or better yet have one come to your fly, then you have been blessed. If that's not enough...

9
The Golden Stone

STONE NYMPHS

I had just finished gathering a set of insect samples with my kick net. I was holding the bugs in some water in a little white collecting dish. There were a number of small mayflies plus one or two larger stone nymphs in the sample. For some reason, I got interrupted and left the dish sitting on a nearby picnic table. I wasn't gone more than a few minutes, but when I came back all the smaller insects were gone. I was puzzled. What could have happened? The specimens couldn't possibly have jumped out of the dish on their own. Still, all that remained were a few large golden stonefly nymphs. When I looked more closely, the stoneflies almost seemed to be smiling. One of them still had an insect leg hanging out of its mouth. They were quite happy with the meal I had left for them. Suddenly, I realized what kind of a predator these nymphs actually are.

The mottled, brown nymphs of the golden stonefly roam the bottom freely, feeding on any hapless insect that crosses their path. They are like the Tyrannosaurus Rex of the river world. Considering their ferocity and their numbers, it's somewhat surprising there are any other insects left.

These golden stones are a major feature of the aquatic life system. The nymphs have a three-year life cycle from egg to adult. Even as one brood is hatching, there are at least two generations of nymphs left in the river. They represent one of the few food items that are available to the trout, in good numbers, all year long. The size of the bug (close to two inches long) means there's lots of food value in each insect so fish will naturally move farther to capture the extra calories. These nymphs are a staple of the trout's diet, something the fish have come to know and rely on.

That's why imitations of these nymphs are one of the most popular flies anywhere in the west. They catch fish just about any time of year. As an added benefit, artificial stonefly nymphs are large enough to hide a good deal of weight. These heavy nymphs will sink right to the bottom, even in swift water. Anglers often use a two fly system to fish down deep. The first fly is a large, weighted stonefly intended to sink the system. The second point fly is smaller, designed to match whatever the current hatch might be. It's a method that works almost anywhere and both flies will catch fish, doubling the chances for success.

THE LINGERING HATCH

Like so many other things on the Metolius, the golden stone hatch is atypical. Generally, you would think of these insects, and their cousins the slightly larger salmonfly, as being a spring hatch of fairly short duration, lasting fifteen or twenty days at the most. On the Metolius, it's different; the hatch is delayed and extended. It begins right before the Fourth of July and lingers all summer, extending through August and on into early September.

The best populations of golden stones inhabit the river in a manner just opposite that of the green drakes. They're mostly found above the thermocline in the warmer water from the head spring down to Jack Creek. There are still fishable numbers in the canyon above the hatchery, but once downstream of the hatchery they are quite limited until you get well downriver near the Horn of the Metolius.

Prior to the hatch, the golden stone nymphs migrate toward the bank. At selected sites along the river they congregate, waiting to ripen and hatch. If you can find one of these pre-hatch colonies, there will be hundreds of nymphs gathered under the rocks. At the appropriate time, under the cover of darkness, the insects crawl out of the river up onto the bank and hatch. I've gone down at midnight with a flashlight to watch them arch their backs, split their shucks, and wiggle free. The newly emerged adults move off and hide deep in the bushes, where they strengthen their wings and rest.

For a brief period, just after the emergence has begun, there will be significant numbers of insects hidden in the bushes, but there is very little sign of them flying in the air or crawling about. You have to look down by the roots of the plants to find them. Yet somehow, during this time, with no sign of the insects on the water, the fish become keyed. They will take dry stonefly patterns aggressively.

After this brief warm-up, the hatch settles into a more normal routine. The insects come out of hiding in the grass. On warmer days, egg-laying adults will be seen in the air all up and down the river corridor. Often, they mistakenly oviposit their eggs on the highways or in parking lots. Something in their tiny insect brains tells them the dark ribbon of asphalt is actually moving water.

THE BANKS AND UNDERCUTS

At this point, the hot-selling fly in the Camp Sherman store will be any kind of floating stonefly pattern that the angler can get his or her hands on. Fishing these flies, however, is not as straight-forward as one might think. The golden stone is not really a hatch, in the true sense of the word. The insects are not emerging mid-water like a mayfly or a caddis and the egg laying adults don't get on the water very much, either. They tend to drop their eggs from up high or just bounce the tip of the abdomen on the water to release them. This means there's very little available to the trout in the normal way we think of bugs and hatches. It's more appropriate to think of these insects as land-based. They're already hatched and just crawling about, so it's more like terrestrial activity. The interface point is not in mid-stream but along the bank near the edge of the river.

Stoneflies of all types are notoriously clumsy crawlers that tend to lose their grip and fall quite often, creating a steady trickle of insects that drop from the bushes onto the water. This is what the fish line up and key on. The standard advice is to cast along the banks and up under the overhanging trees and avoid fishing mid-water altogether.

The undercuts along the edge of the river further contribute to this axiom. The plant communities on the Metolius are so well fed and so thick that they create an extremely dense root mass. I am really not sure whether this root mass is growing out over the river, or whether the river is undercutting it. Either way, there are caverns underneath the water plants at the edge of the river that may go three or four feet back under the bank. In many places, you can put your whole arm under without reaching the back of the cavern.

These undercuts are so well hidden from on top, you would never guess they are there. The strength of the root mass and its resilience are remarkable. You can get out of the river, jump on the bank, and not feel the least bit of flexing. It's easy to see how we can be fooled into thinking it's solid earth under our feet rather than roots and water.

These undercuts are ideal fish habitat. The current is much slower and there is plenty of overhead protection. Fish can move up and down the river and get away from a potential enemy without ever coming out of hiding. They just sit under the edge of the bank, with their belly on the gravel and their back in the roots, and wait for food. They don't have to fear anything. The conveyor of the river will bring them dinner.

When you fish in this type of situation, your casting is blind, you will not know where the trout are and you seldom see rises. The actual event of an insect falling in is random enough that it is difficult to observe. You simply cast, trusting in the attractive power of your golden stone imitation, knowing it's a good motivator of fish. You'll be casting, drifting your fly along, making sure the wing is brushing the bank and maybe even thinking, "Boy this doesn't look all that fishy, it's way too shallow", when out from under the bank a fish will make a swirl. It's so sudden and startling you'll often have the fish hooked up before you realize your fly is gone. In shallow water, the fight is on.

Once out of the upper river's hatch zone, things are less consistent. Summer brings on a smorgasbord of insects with a variety of hatches of small mayflies, caddis, and even some odd stoneflies here and there. While none of these hatches stand out, collectively they can make for some pretty good fishing. I have a series of random memories, one time with little brown stoneflies, another time with mid-size mayflies. Sometimes it happens late in the evening, other times it's midday in the eddies. It's up to you to find your own moment.

I leave home with a well-stocked fly box and I don't tie on anything before I get to the river. It's not like the green drake hatch or the golden stone, where fishing is so predictable you could go to the river with half a dozen flies in a film can. In summer, you may bump into a particular form of activity, have a great day, and then not see that hatch again for years. It's a type of fishing that tests your skills as an observer.

THE OSPREY

One of the best river observers is the osprey. Their hawk calls echo in the forest as they circle above the water. Sometimes I call back, "Hello my friend." I always like it when these magnificent white and brown birds are hunting and I can enjoy their company on the river.

Every so often, if you're really lucky, you'll see one dive and catch a fish. Sometimes they drop right from a perch, other times it's on the wing. They hover, stalling out and getting lined up, then suddenly they fold their wings and plunge. The strike drives them deep into the water where they hit in that classic pose, talons outstretched and their wings folded high over their head. For a split second, most of the bird goes underwater, leaving a shower of spray. Then they lift with a powerful stroke, swimming upward with their first few wing beats.

The ospreys don't get a fish on every try. Sometimes they go back in the air dejected, while other times, when they're lucky, they get a nice size trout and the bird struggles with the weight, trying to lift it off the water. They barely make it airborne, just clearing the surface of the river as they go. Almost immediately, they adjust the fish with their feet so that instead of carrying it sideways in the wind they turn it, lining it up head first, like a bomb underneath a fighter plane.

Once clear of the river, they shake to get rid of the excess water. In midflight they shudder from head to toe just like a wet dog. The wiggle goes right down to end of the tail and you can see the spray flying in the sunshine. Why they don't just drop out of the sky, I'll never know.

As the bird flies off it calls to its mate, who is usually not too far away, and she comes circling in with a responding call. They're talking to one another and I imagine they're saying something like "Honey, I got dinner." They fly off toward the nest to share with their young, calling as they go.

The ospreys often have favorite perches along the river. These dead limbs or snags give them a roost high above the water where they can sit and watch. From these high vantage points, the birds can see better than we do down at river level. They have a better angle looking down into the water, avoiding all the reflections, glare and surface disturbances that blind us at the surface. This visual advantage helps them discover where trout are lying. It's their hunting tool and their method.

Over the years, I've adopted the osprey's technique and have found quite a few perches of my own. Any time I can get to a high spot above the river or above a pool, I climb up and spend some time watching. It's really quite educational when you take time out to watch fish and to observe them without disturbance; it can be as much fun as actually trying to catch them.

PREY IMAGE

Friends sometimes accuse me of having fish eyes; they say I have trout painted on the inside of my glasses. Scientists say what I've done is develop a prey image. All predator species, including humans, can develop the skills to see and sense their prey. We learn to break down natural camouflage and to see a prey image according to the species we most commonly hunt.

As an example, I am constantly impressed by the number of animals a good deer hunter can spot up on a steep hillside. They will see large herds where I see only sagebrush. It isn't until we get to the river that the tables are turned and my prey image takes over. Here, I have learned to play a game of watery illusion. I've learned it is not fish you are looking for but the clues that give fish away. Seldom do you see a whole trout plainly; it's really only a hint of his image that you are looking for. You see your quarry through fish-like shapes, passing glances and incomplete images.

There are many clues. Sometimes it will be a patch of color that's not right. Fish have outstanding color camouflage but it's not perfect. After you have seen this slightly odd shade, your eye becomes accustomed to it. It's one clue that says, "Look here for a trout." At other times, the give-away will be the fish's fins. The white leading edge of the pectoral fins is like the tail of a deer, a very distinctive mark, and just the rippling of the fins is a give-away. The shadow of the fish is yet another clue. When the light is right, you'll see a fish shape moving back and forth over the bottom, even though you might not see the trout at all.

After you pick up a hint or a clue, if you study that area long enough you'll get a fuller view, enough of a glimpse to confirm or deny what it is that you thought you saw in the beginning. In this way, fish watching becomes a game of trying to make sense out of ever-shifting patterns of light and shade.

Once your skill is developed, it will seem so natural that you'll start to take your abilities for granted. I will see a fish and point it out to a friend and he'll stare, strain, and not see a thing. I think to myself, "How could you not see that? It's so obvious." In the end I have to point out where the fish is. We may spend several minutes trying to distinguish different shaped rocks and odd sand patches in order to pin down the location. Sure enough, after a while the breakthrough finally occurs. In a flash of insight he'll cry out, "Oh, I see it!" and my friend is on the way to building his own prey image for the future.

As you build your prey image, there will be many small epiphanies along the way like one day when I was fishing in the canyon. I climbed onto a hillside so I could search a pool (osprey-like) for some larger rainbows that I knew inhabited this particular stretch of river. I was studying the water for quite some time, fifteen minutes or more, when suddenly I saw a fish. I have no idea what keyed my eye to him, a change in the light, a flat spot in the current? Suddenly he was there, right in plain sight.

It was an interesting holding lie. The river bottom in this pool was sandy and there were several rocks scattered randomly in midstream. In the eddy area behind each one the river had left a dark, streamlined deposit of bark and pine needles, like a series of teardrops on the river bottom. A fish had nosed up over one of these deposits and was resting in the current break, his color and shape a perfect match with the surroundings. He was in plain sight and yet he was nearly invisible. When I finally got his image, I had to do a double-take to make sure I was really seeing a trout.

After that first breakthrough, I was suddenly able to see other fish in similar locations. Before the day was done, I saw half a dozen nice fish in these teardrop lies and over the next few weeks I started seeing more and more fish. Gradually, from that single moment, I was able to expand and develop my vision. My prey image was one level sharper.

The Heron

Eventually, just watching fish isn't enough and I have to get down to the river and start stalking the trout. Then the heron becomes my role model. He is the bird whose fishing style is most like our own. He wades and fishes, approaching his prey with stealth and silence until just the right moment.

Herons are majestic birds with a certain style, but it's hard to observe them very closely. They don't like people very much. Most of my encounters on the Metolius are fleeting glances as the birds fly away just at the moment I come into sight. It is rare when I get a chance to fish near one and I consider it a special privilege.

When they are across the river posing with one foot in the air they will, at first, seem stationary, but if

you watch long enough you'll discover that they are moving very slowly. You'll see a bird in one spot, standing still, then look at him five minutes later and he's twenty feet away, still looking as if he hasn't moved a muscle. He is so careful and so deliberate with his movements it's like watching the hands of a clock go around. He blends so completely that the fish don't even know he is there.

While none of us will ever achieve the stealth of a heron, the lesson is still valuable. It suggests that fish don't actually see the heron, they only see his movement. They don't know he's there unless he's foolish enough to ruffle a wing. Similarly, fish don't see us as a clear image of a human being standing on the stream bank, either. The lens of the river surface distorts both ways so we don't see the fish clearly but they can't see us clearly either. Movement is what gives us away.

This doesn't mean, however, that you have to be absolutely still while fly fishing. In nature, there is a good deal of movement all around the stream: wind in the pines, the ruffling of the brush. Fish see this kind of activity all the time. If our movements blend with the movements of nature, in a slow, deliberate fashion we can make ourselves disappear in much the same way the heron does; we hide in plain sight.

In his book *Dry Flies*, Gary LaFontaine says that after a fly angler initially disturbs the water with his entry, it will take eight to ten minutes for the trout to come back around. After that, if you wade slowly and move quietly in a steady, rhythmic way that makes you blend in, you can just fish right amongst the trout; they will not react in an adverse way. It's only when you make a sudden, sharp movement that they spook and scatter.

I call the skill of learning to move like this, getting down to river speed. In our day-to-day lives, we live in a pretty hectic world. Horns honking, cars speeding – everybody with some place to be and nobody on time. If we bring that to the river, the fish run like crazy. On the other hand, if we do what we really came to do, which is relax, settle down and make time irrelevant, then we enter an almost Zen-like state. The life of the river moves in around us and we have a chance to connect. We find ourselves gradually discovering peace, harmony, and maybe a few simple trout on the line as well.

10
The Bull Trout

THE OTHER NATIVE

Bull trout are often considered to be "the other" native fish in the Metolius. Their life history and behaviors have always set them apart. They never have been really popular with fishermen for several reasons. They are fierce predators and have often been perceived as competing with us for fish we would like to catch, ourselves. They also don't respond well to traditional fishing methods – they won't take a dry fly – so anglers have to use heavy gear and special tactics with bigger rods and weighted flies. Not everyone is interested. To each his own, I guess.

I love the bull trout. I think it is one of the most interesting and unusual fresh water fishes anywhere in North America. Its size alone sets it apart. The average fish is five to eight pounds. Bigger ones in the ten to fifteen pound class are fairly common and the trophies are twenty pounds or more. For a fresh water fish that doesn't go to the ocean like a salmon, these are big animals. Biologists think some day a world record could be caught out of the Metolius. This would be a fish of more than thirty-two pounds.

Size alone is not what makes them intriguing. Almost everything about their habits and behavior is unusual. For starters, they are not true trout; they're in a closely related family called char. The char are distinct from true trout in that they have very fine scales and a reversed spotting pattern – light on dark background. Brook trout and lake trout are also members of the char family.

At first glance, bull trout may strike you as rather plain looking fish. They don't have a lot of distinct markings. Their colors vary quite a bit, ranging anywhere from almost black to a very light bronze color. The fish are darker over the back, shading to light tan or buff under the belly. They have faint lemon spots. In the sunlight, their fine scales give them an almost metallic sheen. That's when you'll start to see the beauty in their coloration. It's a lot like looking at a desert landscape; empty at first, but the more you look, the more you see.

APEX PREDATOR

Bull trout are absolutely at the top of the food chain. They're classed as a piscivor, a fish eater who makes a living devouring its neighbors. They have almost no natural enemies other than humans. A bear might be able to get one occasionally and an otter might try, but I think that would be pretty much an even wrestling match. Otherwise, there is nothing out there that would even attempt to take one.

You can see how secure the fish are in a resting lie. I have been able to sneak up close enough to be able to reach out underwater and touch them with my rod tip. If you did that to a trout, they would absolutely explode with panic. The bull trout simply moves over a bit and treats the rod tip as a minor annoyance showing no sign of panic or fear at all.

Bull trout are well adapted for their niche in the world. They have a large head and a big mouth with a good set of teeth. They're not fangs, like sharks teeth, but don't be deceived. Though small, these teeth are wickedly sharp and there are lots of them. I've had enough lacerations on my hands, taking hooks out, that I have developed a healthy respect.

When they go on the feed, bull trout can be extremely aggressive, making for a kind of on-going story around Camp Sherman. An unsuspecting angler will hook a rainbow and the ensuing struggle alerts a bull trout. Like a shark on a blood trail, the bull will close in, thinking he has an easy dinner. All of a sudden, the hapless angler has a huge behemoth from the deep swirling at the hooked trout on the end of his line. It makes for great fishing stories.

If the bull trout actually succeeds in getting hold of the fish, it's even better. Bulls are like a junkyard dog that bites down and hangs on to the bitter end. They hit, trying to make a killing blow, but sometimes their targets are large enough they don't always succeed. Dinner is often still pretty active, so bull trout just use their powerful jaws to hang on. By holding their victim sideways in the current, they cut off the flow of water over its gills. Eventually their prey drowns and they're able to turn it and swallow it whole, head first.

If a bull trout manages to get hold of a fish that's on the end of a fly line, it's a spectacular event. The angler is likely to be convinced the bull has swallowed his rainbow or somehow gotten itself hooked on the fly. The fight goes all the way to the end. The bull trout will be rolling up on its side with exhaustion and the angler will be reaching out, thinking he has caught a trophy. At the last second, the bull will let go, returning a somewhat mangled trout to the angler. The startled fisherman hardly knows how to react. It's a great story, but it's not likely to be believed anywhere very far outside of Camp Sherman and the immediate Metolius area.

THE DECLINE

It's now thought that, in the early 1980's, bull trout came very close to extinction in the Metolius. Spawning ground counts done about that time show the population was so small they were on the very edge of viability. There are many reasons why this deterioration was allowed to go to this extent, but neglect and misunderstanding are probably tops on the list. The nature of the bull trout, as an aggressive predator, doesn't win it many friends. For a long time, it was widely believe they were responsible for significant damage to both trout and salmon populations.

These beliefs were so firmly held that, at on time, the state of Oregon had a bounty on bull trout and paid people to kill them. On the Metolius, they pitch-forked them up onto the bank, trying to get rid of them. This was in the days before the dam, when the salmon could still get into the river. Fish and Wildlife workers used to set up a weir and capture salmon for an egg-take so young salmon could be reared in the hatchery. Unfortunately, the weir set-up was quite close to a major bull trout spawning tributary. The bulls would wander into the weir and get caught, and it was automatically assumed they were following the salmon trying to get eggs. The workers pitch-forked them out of the trap and threw them on the bank to die.

This was done without any real knowledge of the species at all, as most of the research was focused on other, more desirable fishes. The bull trout were left on their own and were not even identified as a distinct species until 1976. Before that, they were called dolly varden trout. Taxonomically, they were simply lumped in with another fairly closely related species. Only in recent years has any serious study been done on them.

THE RECOVERY

I wish I could say the recovery of the bull trout was some grand plan that we all engaged in, but it was not. It was pure accident, the result of a happy coincidence. When the fin-clipped rule went into effect and they started marking all the hatchery trout, bull trout became a catch and release species. Nobody had considered this. We didn't discuss it. There was no plan to benefit the bull trout, yet they were able to take advantage of their new status better than other fishes.

Bull trout are a very long-lived fish. They may survive twenty years or more as compared to six or eight years for a typical rainbow trout. When people started releasing all the larger bull trout, it meant there was an immediate impact on the size of the spawning population. The bull trout also had a competitive advantage. Their niche in life causes them to seek out spring fed tributaries with water temperatures near 40°F in which to spawn and lay eggs. None of the other fish can tolerate water that cold, so the young bull trout grew up in their own little sheltered and protected environment. They have virtually no competition from other fish for either food or habitat.

This cold water slows growth so the young bull trout develop slowly, but by the time they are ready to drop down into the main river, they are tough little customers. They are small, river wise, hardened little fish. They're like a kid that was held back in school for a year, who is older and tougher for their size. They enter the river as the bullies of the playground and grow quickly. It's not long until they start showing signs of their predatory nature.

With the advantage of the young living outside the mainstream, repeated stockings of hatchery trout had virtually no effect on the bull trout population. They thrived while the rainbows where still suffering and their populations began to improve, long before the other species entered recovery.

THE OLD TIMERS

Not everybody was pleased with the success of the bull trout. At first, there was a lot of bad blood. Those who really liked the stocking program didn't understand the bull trout at all and there was a regular weekly battle going on.

The hatchery truck would come by on Friday to one of the popular stocking spots, Allingham Bridge. There are several campgrounds nearby and a very fishable pool below the bridge, so the stocking truck would always finish its rounds here, and put some extra fish in this handy spot. The old guys knew this and would start gathering early on the bridge, like a row of vultures hanging out, waiting.

You would almost think the bull trout had the routine worked out, too. They'd be under the bridge waiting as well; for them, the hatchery trout were an excellent meal. The latter were dumped in the river unprepared, unaware, off-color, uncamouflaged and unadapted. It was like leading lambs to the slaughter and amounted to inviting the bull trout to a free meal.

The hatchery worker would come down from the truck with his scoop of fish. He'd dump them into the river, and before the old guys could get their flies off the hook keeper the bull trout would close in. In a matter of seconds there would be three, four, or five fish sitting on the bottom, each with a struggling hatchery trout cross-wise in its mouth. The old men would be cursing. They blamed the bull trout rather than themselves for the depletion of the river.

A Pebble in a Pond

As the bull trout population improved, it was like dropping a small pebble in a pond. The rings spread outward on the still water and the impact went far and wide. There was an excellent biologist named Don Ratliff who was doing some research on the Metolius right about the time the fin-clipped rule went into effect. He was able to document the improved spawning success and rapidly growing bull trout populations. This was the first time there had ever been any success in enhancing a bull trout population. Word of this work spread in the scientific community and the Metolius became a little epicenter for bull trout awareness. Our recovering population became a model.

All sorts of new research ensued and scientists began to document the significant decline of the bull trout throughout its historic range. An annual meeting was set up, and people interested in bull trout recovery began to gather and exchange information. The fish was soon identified as a species of interest with the Forest Service and the Department of Fish and Wildlife. Other recovery plans were set in motion and eventually the bull trout became listed as a threatened species with the Federal Government.

On the Metolius, the cold springs feeding the small creeks on the west side of the river proved to be ideal bull trout habitat. Our population has continued to grow and flourish. Today, it is widely considered one of the best examples of a healthy bull trout population anywhere in the world.

FALSELY ACCUSED

In their recovered state, Metolius bull trout haven't had a negative impact on other species, and rainbows and bulls seem to co-exist nicely. It's become widely accepted that whitefish, not trout, are the bull's main diet. Whitefish, a non-game species found in most western rivers, are abundant in the Metolius. They eat food similar to trout, but with a much smaller, sucker-like mouth, which vacuums insects from between rocks. They are bottom feeders, not as slim or as fast as a trout and much easier prey for bull trout.

When you find pods of bull trout resting in the deep pools, you also find schools of whitefish. The bulls never go far from their prime food source. The whitefish, in turn, testify to the symbiosis. Many have scars and bite marks from their close encounters. Watching the two species together, you can see that they have co-existed for a long time, almost like lions and wildebeest. Whitefish know every movement of the bull trout, and can sense if their attackers are feeding or resting. At times, the whitefish will sit completely unconcerned, inches away from the nose of a non-feeding bull trout. Other times, when the bull trout are moving, they flee in terror.

I know one pool where you can predict if you're going to get a hit from a bull trout just by watching the whitefish. In this spot, the whitefish sit closer over the sand while the bull trout sit further out over the gravel. If you swing a fly through to the bull trout, out in that darker water, you can't see it very well. Watch the whitefish and you can tell what's going on. As soon as a bull trout moves toward your fly the whitefish will see him and react. They come scurrying by your feet and seconds later the bull trout hits your fly.

It now appears that bull trout focus on trout or salmon only when seeking an alternate food source. If a fish gives off signs of weakness, if it has been injured, or if it is giving off signals of alarm, then the bull trout will respond. They're looking for easy prey and attack hatchery trout or fish on the end of a line. They're just doing what bull trout do, cleaning up the sickness and injury and insuring the survival of the fittest.

All those years the bull trout were vilified, they were not doing any harm at all; they were only serving as a scapegoat for our own greedy intentions. It's pretty interesting how far off the mark we can get and how misinterpreted a species can become. Every time I see pods of bull trout sitting in the pools, it does my heart good. It's a thrilling sight to see that many trophy fish gathered all at once and I can't help but be thankful.

I only hope the bull trout story is heard and that future generations learn from it. We came awfully close to losing something very precious. Worst of all, no one even knew. It wasn't until after the fact that we realized how depleted the population had become. The Metolius wouldn't be the same if we didn't have bull trout anymore.

11
Hatches of September

TILT OF THE PLANETS

The end of summer in the Metolius Basin is an overnight event. One day you're struggling through the heat of the dog days of August. The air is thick and heavy, fishing is slow and it seems more profitable to sit in the water than to fish in it. The fly line probes lazily, the loops seem to struggle through the air, and the fly falls heavily. A snooze under a shady pine is much more inviting than casting to a reluctant trout. Then, overnight, there is a shift. You smell the difference more than see it through some dramatic change of the weather. It's just a sense, like a cooling in your nostrils, that says fall is here. It's such a subtle change it would be easy to doubt your own senses, but the river will not allow that. The day you smell fall in the air, a whole new set of insects will appear. They testify that the planets have tilted, the seasons have changed, and the natural world has moved on.

The fall fishing is superb. In part, that's because the fishing is good everywhere. The crowds dissipate. Anglers are Steelheading, fishing for salmon on the coast or enjoying themselves up on the high mountain lakes. Hunting draws off another group, creating a level of privacy that doesn't exist at other times of the year. There are days when you can have miles of river all to yourself.

The variety of hatches makes it's hard to choose which one is the best. There's a very interesting pale stonefly, sometimes called a willow fly, which is a sister species to the golden stone. It's light tan on the underbelly with very dark blue/black color on the sides, back and wings. This is an evolving species. The wings are often crumpled and malformed. At least half the specimens are flightless; something is telling them they don't need wings anymore. The females often show a bright neon purple egg mass at the end of the abdomen. It is a remarkable psychedelic color and there are not many things like it in nature.

The fall green drake hatch appears just about the same time as the stonefly. These insects are a little bit smaller than the traditional spring drakes, but the impact on the fish is just about the same. With green drake hatches sandwiched on either end of the season, the Metolius enjoys one of the longest green drake hatches anywhere. These insects provide outstanding fishing for close to three months out of the year.

A third hatch I always like in the fall is the tiny green/brown stonefly. Most stoneflies are an inch to an inch and a half long at maturity but these insects are not more than a quarter of an inch long. They're so small they're often mistaken for caddis. They have an odd habit of floating long distances on the water, beating their wings. They make no effort to escape, they just float and flap. It's like wearing a sign that says to the trout, "Free Lunch". It's hard to understand how the behavior benefits the species in the long run.

FALL COLORS

Not long after that first whiff of fall comes along there will be a brief stormy period. The long drought of summer cracks and a little bit of cool, moist weather passes through. After that, we start to drop into the more traditional fall cycle of warm days and cooler nights called Indian Summer.

The green begins to fade along the river and harvest gold takes over. The plants lighten up gradually with more and more yellow showing through each day. Everything is going to seed. The lupines have odd little pea pods, the cow parsnips make broad seed heads and the little blue forget-me-nots turn into nasty little burs that stick to everything.

The color of the water darkens once again as the light angle becomes more oblique. You can't see into it as well; there's less blue/green and more black. Here and there, a patch of vine maples turns red, yellow and gold to punctuate the scene.

It has always intrigued me that the fish seem to change color, too and match the season. Spring rainbows are green and gold like fresh spring plants. In the fall the colors deepen, there is more red and yellow with touches of black in the background. If you bring a fish onto the bank and lay it in the fall leaves, just before you release, it matches perfectly. It's as if one part of the season reflects the other.

THE KOKANEE

Kokanee are known as "the little red fish," a land-locked form of the sockeye salmon. They are anywhere from twelve to fifteen inches long. They use Lake Billy Chinook as their ocean and come back up the Metolius each fall to spawn. The first ones start to arrive right at the change of the season. As they enter the river, they go through a rapid series of changes. In the lake, as young fish, they are silvery bright. By the time they are ready to enter the river, they have turned dark, almost black. Once into the moving water, they quickly start to develop a deep red spawning color. The males get a humped back and curved lower jaw that comes up and forward into an ugly fighting tool called a kype. The kokanee march up-river in little pods or schools, sometimes four or five fish in a group, sometimes fifteen or twenty. They follow the edge of the river, ducking behind the rocks, picking their way along. They move at a steady pace, not pausing or taking breaks; they're feeling the mating urge pulling them forward.

Before the dam, there were some true sockeye salmon in the Metolius. They came up the river, into a tributary called Lake Creek, up through Suttle Lake, and then into Link Creek to spawn. Sockeye require a lake in the river system as part of their life history so these young salmon would rear in Suttle Lake for a period before they moved out to the ocean. Sometime in the late 1930's or 40's, a small dam was built to raise the level of the lake. Although this dam was only about eight feet high, it created an effective barrier and the sockeye run was lost. The species was reintroduced to the system in the late 60's after the reservoir was built. The smaller, freshwater form of the salmon no longer have access to the ocean, so they spawn in the Metolius and then drop down to Billy Chinook to rear and grow.

MEP-TOE-LAS

When the kokanee finally reach the upper river, where the best spawning beds are, they almost immediately go to work digging nests. The hens roll up on their sides, beat their tails on the gravel and dig out a little hollow or depression. Even before they are ready to lay eggs, their bodies begin to decay. Large white fungus patches appear on both the males and females. As with salmon everywhere, they are dying as they spawn.

This process looks rather grizzly. Once the eggs are laid, the fungus really takes over and fish swim in the shallows in all stages of decay. The females sometimes lose their whole tail from digging; other fish go completely blind with white fungus patches covering their entire head and face. These dying fish are so slow you can catch them with your bare hands, if you really want to touch them. Soon the whole river bottom is littered with the white carcasses and in years when there is a big spawn the river smells from the decay.

Interestingly enough, that's the name of the river, Metolius, or in the Indian language, Mep-toe-las, meaning "white fish" or "stinking fish" river, "the place of salmon". Of course, for the Indians it was Chinook salmon causing the stink, not miniature freshwater sockeye, but the effect and the appearance were a lot alike. For a long time, it used to bother me that a place like the Metolius should be called the stinking fish river. That's kind of a nasty name for such a beautiful place. Now I don't think the Indians really meant it quite the way it sounds in our language. Native Americans can be very literal and abrupt in the way they speak. I think they were seeing something more than simply a dead fish when they used that name.

The death of the salmon is the ultimate act of parenting. The nutrients these fish carcasses provide is like a shot in the arm to the health of the river. It's like spreading a garden with a dose of fish emulsion; everything benefits and grows. Plants and algae bloom, which in turn benefits the insects. Even the bull trout get in on the feast. They are just coming out of their own spawn and they line up, devouring the bits of kokanee meat as they float down the river.

The cycle insures the health of the river just before it goes into winter. It guarantees that in ninety to one hundred days, when the small kokanee minnows swim up out of the gravel where the eggs were deposited, there will be plenty for them to eat. The river will be healthy and robust, and they will thrive. This is perhaps closer to how the Indians saw the cycle. Not so much as the river of dead and dying salmon, not so much as the stinking fish river, but more as the place where the cycle of life goes forward. The river of richness and abundance, the place where the salmon thrive.

12
Salmon – Then & Now

THE RUN

I wish I could have seen the river when the salmon were still here in all their glory. It would have been quite a sight. Perhaps it's not all that hard to imagine. There are reports saying it wasn't that much different from present day Chinook runs on the Deschutes below the dams.

The fish came onto the redds, or nest sites, late in the year, probably around mid-October. They would have entered the river earlier, anytime from mid-summer on, but they stayed pretty much to the deep holes where they were well hidden. Most people didn't even know they were around, so they offered very little fishing opportunity.

When they finally came into shallow water and onto nests, they were well advanced into spawning decay. The fungus spots, which develop quickly, would have started showing almost immediately. According to one outdoor writer for the Oregonian newspaper, you could hear the fish at night, splashing about on the nests. Fish the size of salmon in a small river would have created quite a ruckus and done some serious excavation of the river bottom. A twenty or thirty pound Chinook salmon builds a nest the size of a bathtub. The digging would have reshaped the gravel in some of the better spawning riffles, creating large wash boards and rolls in the river bottom.

THE DAMS

They say the run was in decline even before the dams went into place. Pressures in the ocean fishery and canneries at Astoria, near the mouth of the Columbia River, had already taken a toll, but hydropower was the straw that broke the camel's back.

There are two dams in the Pelton/Round Butte Complex that created the problem. They were both constructed on the Deschutes River. The upper dam, Round Butte, flooded back upstream putting the mouths of the Crooked River, The Upper Deschutes and the Metolius all under water.

In the original design, there was a plan to get fish around the complex, but it didn't work quite the way it was drawn up. The huge fish ladder on the lower dam (Pelton) was close to three-quarters of a mile long. Apparently, it functioned properly for a year or two while the second dam was still under construction. When Round Butte dam was closed, the designers used a less conventional approach to fish passage. They planned to take adult fish upstream, over the dam, with a cable-car like device. The fish would come into a trap at the base of the dam and then were automatically given a ride on a ski lift-like gondola some 250 feet up over the face of the dam. Surprisingly, this Rube Goldberg contraption actually worked, and they were successful in getting the returning adult fish back up-river.

The small, out-migrating salmon smolts proved to be another matter. The downstream trapping device I can only describe as a giant toilet bowl. There was a pipe placed up the face of the dam, and at the top there was a box or a trap. When a full load of fish was captured, a valve at the bottom was opened. The water column would be gradually lowered and the fish carried down. They were being flushed, ever so gently, right down the tube.

With twenty/twenty hindsight, we now know the system failed because the designers didn't use enough attractive water at the top of the dam to show the fish the way. Out-migrating salmon travel at or near the surface of the river, following the currents downstream. The Round Butte dam takes its water into the turbines at the base of the dam some 200 feet down. The main flow of the river, over 40,000 cfs, is down at the bottom of the reservoir. The passage facilities at the surface only spilled 15 cfs to show the fish the way to go. It was as if the fish came into the lake riding on a fire hose and they were looking for a tiny little squirt gun to show them the way out. The young fish wandered in the reservoir, confused by the mixing currents of three great rivers. Cold water from the Metolius would dive under warmer water from the other two streams. The little smolts didn't know where to go and there wasn't enough out-flow to show them the way to the sea.

For a few years, there was an effort to trap fish and truck them. This proved ineffective and in 1968 the run was abandoned. Fish & Wildlife started relying on hatchery reared fish as replacements below the dam and quit operating the passage facility altogether.

LOST CONNECTION

More than just the salmon was lost when the dam was built. We lost the interconnectedness of the river system, too. Modern biology is beginning to show us that, where native fish populations are concerned, there are important mixing zones between distinct populations of fish. If you envision a river system as being like the limbs of a tree, each branch is a separate and distinct fish population, but they all connect back to the trunk and the roots. This reconnecting is where the gene pool is freshened and the species is kept healthy and vital.

In a way, fishermen have known about these zones for a long time. You never pass up a confluence pool where two streams come together because they always hold fish in abundance. Larger trout, too. It is an obvious and rich mixing pot where the lives of the two streams swirl together for a moment.

Apparently, the mixing zone where the three rivers came together, which is now at the bottom of Lake Billy Chinook, was one of the best confluence pools of all times. The fishermen with whom I have talked, who were lucky enough to have hiked down into the canyon before the dams were built, speak of the place with great reverence. Their fishing stories are amazing, the stuff of legends.

The operator of the fish trap at Round Butte told a similar story. He talked about all the amazing fish, besides the salmon, that came into the trap in the first few years after the dam was closed. There were huge rainbows and gargantuan bull trout desperately trying to make it through into that mixing zone. Their instinct was telling them to create that all-important genetic and species interchange.

What exactly the long-term impacts of this loss of mixing will be, no one can really say. The individual populations on each river are now fractured, isolated and kept independent and alone. For a while it might not make any difference at all, but long-term there will be a piper to pay.

SALMON RECOVERY

It would be a wonderful dream to see salmon back in the Metolius and not have to imagine anymore what it was like, and to have a river with its connection to the ocean once again restored. It's not entirely a pipe dream anymore. In recent years (mid-1990's), the Pelton/Round Butte Complex has been undergoing scrutiny from the Federal Energy Re-licensing Committee. This is part of a periodic review of all hydro projects. As part of this review, the utility has taken a serious look at the question of fish passage, and have re-opened the concept for further study and review.

As of this writing, the plans under way are to be applauded. The utility Portland General Electric, guided by their biologist Don Ratliff (the same man who helped with the bull trout restoration) has re-introduced young salmon from hatch boxes in the Metolius in order to study their migrating habits. There's a computer model study of currents in the reservoir along with engineering drawings for an elaborate rubber curtain system which would be installed in front of the dam. This would allow some of the water now going through the

turbines to be used to attract fish at the top. If it all works and they can restore passage, it would be a landmark project, perhaps one of the first times ever that a utility has gone to such lengths to repair damage. It could have implications in other fisheries all around the world.

Still, I feel this touch of reluctance, especially when I look back at experiences of the past. Fisheries biology is an infant science, and there is much we do not know. Like so many other things in our society, it's been heavily influenced by outside forces like politics, special interests and jobs. State of the art science is often overlooked or manipulated to meet other ends. It's human nature that once a project of this magnitude is started people will want to see it to the end, no matter what that end may be.

The cause of the salmon is very noble, it can generate great press, but we must keep in mind that these would be restored fish and not the original native fish of the Metolius. There have been many changes to the river system since the dams were built. We don't know things like how the re-introduced chinook salmon would interact with the previously introduced sockeye salmon or kokanee. Is there enough room for all that bio-mass in the river? Especially since so much habitat has been removed in the form of wood material, like the old trees and log jams.

It's not a slam dunk putting the river back the way it was. In many respects we would be engaged in a huge roll of the dice. I hope we don't become like the hatchery managers before us. I hope we are not stepping off into uncharted territory, setting out with the best of intentions for the fish and the river, only to arrive somewhere else altogether.

I don't have the answers and I don't know what the future holds. I only hope we move forward with caution and respect for the river. It's a tall order, to restore salmon. They are a special fish, very spiritual, and they often have minds of their own. The path may not lead exactly where we think it is going to go, but if we can succeed, I barely want to let myself dream what salmon in the Metolius could mean.

13
Late Fall and Winter

SEASONS IN REVERSE

The sequence of hatches through the later part of fall creates an odd reversing of the seasons. During spring and into summer there is a pattern to the hatches, an ordered sequence which is reversed going toward winter. At first it's pretty hectic, with the pale stoneflies and then the green drakes. At that time of year, in September, it's hard to know which way to turn. The kokanee thrashing about can be a huge distraction. You never know whether movement in the water is a feeding trout or just another spawned-out salmon swirling at the surface.

Gradually, as the days grow shorter, the activity slows down. The kokanee are done on the nests and only their carcasses remain. There are still cool nights and pleasant days, but it's not like September when a warm day means summery 80°F temperatures. This is the heart of fall and the October caddis becomes the dominant insect.

These large caddis couldn't be more suited to the season; their black wings and orange bodies celebrate the colors of Halloween. They are so large they are sometimes mistaken for stoneflies, but their distinct loping flight pattern out over the water is a signature movement. They flutter and glide like a meadow lark, lifting and dropping as they go. Anglers sometimes get frustrated during this hatch. An October caddis is a large food item which should attract a lot of attention from the trout but they are quick and agile and not easily trapped on the water, so they don't give the fish as much of an opportunity as it might appear they should. The trout feed only at selected sites, around specific trees and bushes where the caddis form large mating swarms. Here the insect numbers achieve what might be called critical mass when there are enough insects on the water to create a reliable food source and the trout turn to them with relish.

Sometime in late October, Indian summer comes to an end. The seemingly endless sequence of cool nights and pleasant, warm sunny days is over, and the storm clouds gather once again. It's blustery, wet and cold. Halloween is always a perfect night for spooks – dark and rainy. The headlights of your car shine off the rain-soaked pavement but the light is swallowed in the swirling winds and the utter blackness of the night.

Despite stormy weather and afternoons cut short by the loss of daylight savings time, there's still some good fishing well into November. The caddis gradually fade away and all that's left are the prolific small mayfly hatches of the late season. This time of year, even on sunny days, the wood smoke from a nearby cabin seems to settle and hang between the trees in the river corridor. It smells pleasant and inviting, a sharp contrast to the blustery weather outside.

There are often pine needles blown down on the water. The little mayflies get lost in the debris, but somehow the trout seem to know the season is almost over and the year is at an end. They want to gather all the energy they can for the coming winter. They rise freely and with an abandon that is uncommon at other times of the year.

FIRST SNOW

One evening, late in November, the snow begins to fall. The night is still, except for the rumble of the snowplow passing on its rounds. At dawn you awake to a world transformed and the snow clings to the pine bows and sifts down through the trees in soft flakes. The river is transformed too, and the colors are gone. It's now a tableau of black and white and shades of gray. The water is inky black with a silver sheen of snow reflected on its surface. There are little mists rising. Yet, even in the midst of the worst storm, right at the water's edge there is a little band of green where the grass is as bright as if it were spring. This little oasis never goes away because the water temperature, still at 48 °F, fresh from the headspring, warms the ground, leaving a little patch of land that never knows winter.

Beneath the swirling currents, the effect is much the same. The cold-blooded fish are slowed by the cooling temperatures and the lack of sunshine. They won't move as far to take a fly but they are still able to feed and grow. They're not like trout in a lake that go almost catatonic because they're trapped underneath the ice. In fact, this is the time of year when the rainbows come to spawn.

Unlike the kokanee, the rainbow trout are very quiet and very secretive about their arrival in the upper river. They don't seem to gather on redd sites like other spawning fish. You don't see them darting, digging and protecting the nest. Over the years I have walked the river, on occasion, in December, January and February trying to catch pairs on the nests but I have never succeeded. I have never seen a pair of native rainbows actively spawning in the Metolius. The best I can do is find the scattered redd sites where the fish have already deposited their eggs, leaving the distinctive depression and clean, white gravel where the river bottom has been disturbed. I guess it doesn't matter, I really don't need to see the fish. It's enough to know they are there; it's enough to know their numbers have been increasing. I can count more redds than ever before and that does my heart good.

SIGNATURE SPECIES

The rainbows are a special fish for me that I hold dear to my heart for many reasons. Fly fishing has a lot of history surrounding it and the rainbows are an important part of that. They offer classic dry fly fishing in the oldest tradition of the sport. It was with the rainbows and this style of fishing that my career began. They taught me the first lessons about the river and no matter what other species I may encounter, I will always come back to them to cast a dry fly.

Along the way I have learned many lessons. Through the rainbow trout I have come to recognize that no fish species lives in isolation and the health and well being of all the fish populations depends on the health of the whole ecosystem. The Metolius rainbows stand as a shining example of what a few small sacrifices can do to promote a fish species and a healthy ecosystem. They prove that, given a chance, the fish want to survive.

This is a very important concept that I think is often overlooked. On one hand, nature is very frail and very easily disturbed. This idea causes me and others a great deal of concern for what the future might bring. On the other hand, the world of nature can be very tough and very resilient, too. Given any chance at all, continuation of the species is a very powerful urge. Fish are built to survive and if we give them the space to do it they will prosper. Look at the history of it; even when a volcano like Mount Jefferson erupts and spews lava into the river, the fish are able to return and repopulate. They have done it in the past and they could do it again. I find this to be a very powerful and very positive statement. This vision of the future needs only one important ingredient. The river and the rainbows will always need friends and they will always need people looking out for them and speaking up on their behalf. If people care about the native fish and the native rainbows, good things will happen.

In that regard there is great hope. Just the other day I met an angler on the stream, a brand new convert who had just started fly fishing within the last year. Out of the blue, he began to lecture me, telling me, in very emphatic terms, how important the native fish are. He told me how we need to protect more rivers both here in Oregon and throughout the country. I thought to myself, "You go, buddy. You tell 'em how it is."

So, in the cold snow of winter with the flakes settling on my shoulders and my eyebrows, I see the newly formed redds, and I am warm all over. Things are good; the eggs, for another year, are in the gravel and the cycle has started once again.

Appendix

The I PASS Pledge

Seeing fish spawning in the wild is one pay off for the catch and release so many of us have practiced over the years. That's why I am concerned by a growing trend among fishermen to specifically target these fish. I understand the temptation: spawning fish are concentrated, easy to locate and they are defensive of their nest sites. Fishing for them brings great results with large fish.

Unfortunately, as with most thing that are too easy, there is a down side. Spawning fish are weakened and in poor condition. If they are pestered enough, the spawn may be interrupted and only partially completed. On top of that, wading through the nest site to get to the spawning fish can kill eggs and young fry still sheltered in the gravel.

Some might argue these damages are inconsequential. To an extent I might agree; the impacts are certainly not as great as things like overharvest or habitat degradation. Still, targeting spawners is not a healthy practice and should be avoided if for no other reason than to show respect for the fish. That is why I have taken the "I PASS" pledge. It is presented here, for the first time ever.

I PASS is a simple acronym meaning, "I Pledge to Avoid Spawning Sites."

It's pretty straightforward. To take the pledge you must learn to identify spawning areas and if you think you are in one, move away. Look for these signs.

1. Light colored circular patches in the gravel indicating recent disturbance.
2. Small depressions and mounds in the gravel indicating nest sites and eggs.
3. Numbers of fish concentrated in shallow water over a fine gravel bottom.
4. Fish that hug to a site and refuse to move off, even after a disturbance.
5. Fish that are dark and soft and somewhat poorly conditioned.

If you do these things, if you take the I PASS pledge, the fish, the river and future generations of anglers will appreciate your concern.

IPASS
I Pledge to Avoid Spawning Sites

Respect fish.
Move away from spawning areas.
Look for pale circular patches in gravel, depressions and mounds in gravel indicating nests and eggs, fish concentrated in shallow water over gravel, fish hugging a site, dark & poorly conditioned fish.

Conservation

No Nonsense Fly Fishing Guidebooks believes that, in addition to local information and gear, fly fishers need clean water and healthy fish. We encourage preservation, improvement, conservation, enjoyment and understanding of our waters and their inhabitants. While fly fishing, take care of the place, practice catch & release and try to avoid spawning fish.

When you aren't fly fishing, a good way to help all things wild and aquatic is to support organizations dedicated to these ideas. No Nonsense Fly Fishing Guidebooks does and is a member, sponsor of and donor to organizations that preserve what we cherish.

American Fly Fishing Trade Association .... (360) 636-0708	International Women Fly Fishers .... (888) 811-4933
American Rivers .... (202) 547-6900	New Mexico Trout .... (505) 344-6363
Amigos Bravos .... (505) 758-3874	Oregon Trout .... (503) 222-9091
California Trout .... (415) 392-8887	Outdoor Writers Association Of America .... (406) 728-7434
Deschutes Basin Land Trust .... (541) 330-0017	Recreational Fishing Alliance .... (888) JOIN-RFA
Ducks Unlimited .... (901) 758-3825	Theodore Roosevelt Conservation Alliance ...... (877) 770-8722
Federation of Fly Fishers .... (406) 585-7592	Trout Unlimited .... (800) 834-2419
International Game Fish Association .... (954) 941-3474	

Metolius River Basin Accommodations & Services

Metolius Recreation Association
PO Box 64
Camp Sherman, OR 97730
(541) 595-6117
www.metoliusriver.com

Black Butte Resort, RV Park & Motel
25635 SW Forest Service Road 1419
Camp Sherman, OR 97730
(541) 595-6514
www.blackbutte-resort.com

Camp Sherman Store & Fly Shop
PO Box 638
Camp Sherman, OR 97730
(541) 595-6711
www.campshermanstore.com

Cold Springs Resort & RV Park
25615 Cold Springs Resort Ln.
Camp Sherman, OR 97730
(541) 595-6271
www.coldsprings-resort.com

HooDoo Recreation Services
Summer Campgrounds
Winter Skiing & RV Parking
PO Box 20
Sisters, OR 97759
(541) 822-3799
www.hoodoo.com/campgrounds.htm

House On The Metolius
PO Box 100
Camp Sherman, OR 97730
(541) 595-6620

Kokanee Café & Guest Rooms
Camp Sherman, OR 97730
(541) 595-6420

Lake Creek Lodge
13375 SW Forest Service Road 1419
Camp Sherman, OR 97730
(800) 797-6331
Fax: (541) 595-1016
lake@outlawnet.com
www.lakecreeklodge.com

Metolius River Lodge
PO Box 110
Camp Sherman, OR 97730
(800) 595-6290
cabins@metoliusriverlodges.com
www.metoliusriverlodges.com

Metolius River Resort
25551 SW Forest Service 1419
Camp Sherman, OR 97730
(800) 81-TROUT
www.metolius-river-resort.com

Suttle Lake Resort
13300 Hwy 20
Sisters, OR 97759
(541) 595-6662
Fax: (541) 549-0882
mabott10@aol.com
www.centormall.com/
Suttle_Lake_Resort

John Judy Fly Fishing
PO Box 122
Camp Sherman, OR 97730
541-595-2073
Fax 595-5552
johnjudy@outlawnet.com

Campgrounds
Forest Service
Sisters Ranger Station
PO Box 249
Sisters, OR 97759
(541) 549-7700
www.fs.fed.us

USDA Forest Service
Campground Reservations
www.reserveusa.com

Travel & Tourism Resources
Oregon Tourism Commission
775 Summer St. NE
Salem, OR 97301-1282
(503) 373-1270
(800) 547-7842
www.traveloregon.com

Central Oregon Visitors Association
63085 N. Hwy 97
Bend, OR 97701
(541) 382-8334
(800) 800-8334
www.covisitors.com

Sisters Area Chamber of Commerce
PO Box 430
Sisters, OR 97759
(541) 549-4253
www.sisterschamber.com

Licenses & Regulations
Oregon Division of Fish & Wildlife
www.dfw.state.or.us
ODFW High Desert Region
61374 Parallel Road
Bend, OR 97702
(541) 388-6363

BLM Central Oregon Resource Area
3050 NE Third
PO Box 550
Prineville, OR 97754
(541) 416-6700
Fax: (541) 416-6798
www.or.blm.gov

Recommended Reading
No Nonsense Guide to Fly Fishing
Central & Southeastern Oregon
Harry Teel

Slack Line Strategies for Fly Fishing
John Judy

Oregon Atlas & Gazetteer
Delorme

Central Oregon Fly Shops

Camp Sherman Store
25451 Forest Service Rd.
Camp Sherman, OR 97730
(541) 595-6711
www.campshermanstore.com

Cascade Guides and Outfitters
P.O. Box 3676
Sunriver, OR 97707
(541) 593-2358
(888) 230-HOOK
Fax: (541) 593-2380
www.cascadeguides.com

Deschutes Canyon Fly Shop
599 S. Highway 197
PO Box 334
Maupin, OR 97037
(541) 395-2565
www.flyfishingdeschutes.com

Deschutes River Outfitters
61115 S. Highway 97
Bend, OR 97701
(541) 388-8191

Fin'N'Feather
785 West 3rd Street
Prineville, OR 97754
(541) 447-8691

Fly & Field Outfitters
143 SW Century Drive
Bend, OR 97701
(541) 318-1616
www.flyandfield.com

Numb-Butt Fly Fishing
380 N. Highway 26
Madras, OR 97741
(541) 325-5515

Sunriver Fly Shop
Sunriver Business Park
Sunriver, OR 97707
(541) 593-8814

The Fly Box
923 SE Third Street
Bend, OR 97701
(541) 388-3330

The Fly Fisher's Place
151 West Main St.
PO Box 1179
Sisters, OR 97759
(541) 549-3474

The Patient Angler
55 NW Wall Street
Bend, OR 97701
(541) 389-6208

Fly Fishing the Internet
www.fedflyfishers.org
www.flyfishamerica.com
www.intlwomenflyfishers.org
www.tu.org
www.waterworkswonders.org

Weather Service
www.wrh.noaa.gov

Knots
www.earlham.edu/~peters/
knotlink.html

Books
www.nononsenseguides.com
www.globe-pequot.com
www.falconbooks.com

Nearby Fly Fishing

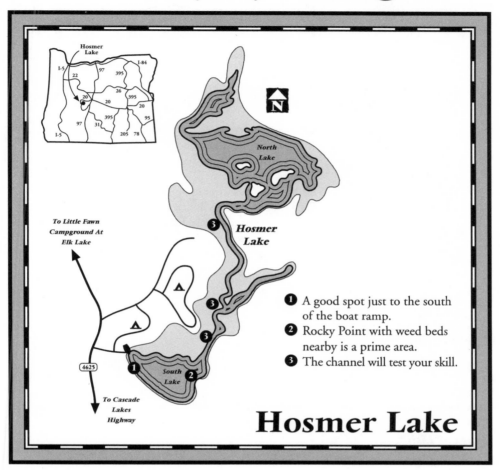

Hosmer Lake

❶ A good spot just to the south of the boat ramp.
❷ Rocky Point with weed beds nearby is a prime area.
❸ The channel will test your skill.

Types of Fish

Good Atlantic salmon and brook trout. Both grow to an average of 16 to 18".

Flies to Use

Dry: Parachute Adams, Comparadun, Parachute Caddis, Goddard Caddis, Tom Thumb, Palomino Midge, Century Drive Midge, Timberline Emerger and Callibaetis.

Nymph: Leech, Stovepipe, Damsel, Scud, Carey Special, Beadhead Serendipity, Zug Bug, Pheasant Tail, Cates Turkey and Water Boatman.

When to Fish

It's a mixed bag of opinions. Some like June-July, while others prefer late September. Most Hosmer fly fishers agree that evening is the best time of the day for any kind of fly fishing.

Season & Limits

Hosmer is open year-round, but snow will keep anglers away between November and May.

Fall River

Map legend:

1. Good water below the falls. Check synopsis for season on this section.
2. Nice section. Fish the undercuts and watch for private property.
3. Fish hatchery, very popular.
4. Good water. You'll earn what you catch. Watch & listen carefully for larger fish rising near deadfalls.
5. The headwaters. A great area all year and a top spot for winter and early spring.

Types of Fish

Rainbow, brook and browns around 12", but keep an eye out for bigger fish.

Flies to Use

Dry: Adams, Renegade, Comparadun, Pale Morning Dun, Blue Winged Olive, Knock Down Dun, Captive Dun, Slow Water, CDC & Elk Hair Caddis, Henryville, Griffith's Gnat, Palomino, Ant Stimulator, Humpy, Madam X, Para-hopper.

Nymph: Pheasant Tail, Prince, Brassie, Serendipity, Hare's Ear, Sparkle Pupa, Zug Bug, Soft Hackle, also all in beadhead.

Streamer: Zonker, Woolly Bugger.

When to Fish

Most Fall River enthusiasts like late June, July and August. Evening hours generally best.

Season & Limits

Artificial flies only, weights (on line or leader) prohibited. April 26 - September 30, open below the falls. Open year round above the falls. Check ODFW synopsis for special regulations.

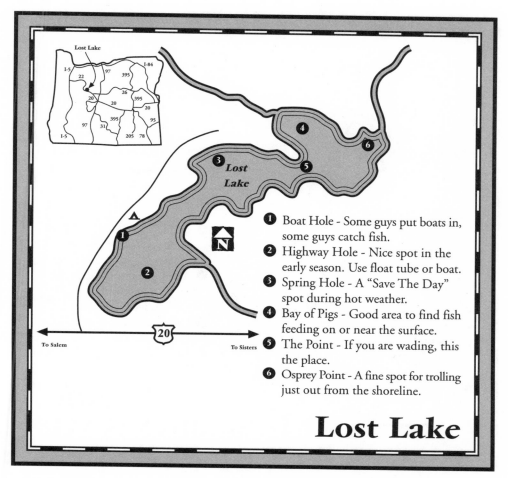

1 Boat Hole - Some guys put boats in, some guys catch fish.

2 Highway Hole - Nice spot in the early season. Use float tube or boat.

3 Spring Hole - A "Save The Day" spot during hot weather.

4 Bay of Pigs - Good area to find fish feeding on or near the surface.

5 The Point - If you are wading, this the place.

6 Osprey Point - A fine spot for trolling just out from the shoreline.

Lost Lake

Types of Fish
Rainbow and brook trout.

Flies to Use
Dry: Callibaetis Parachute and Spinner, Adams Parachute, Comparadun, Timberline Emerger, Captive Dun, Suspender Midge, Griffith's Gnat, Para-midge, Adult Damsel, Black Elk Hair Caddis, Tom Thumb, Goddard Caddis, X Caddis, Ant, Red Tarantula, Float-n-Fool.
Nymph: Beadhead Leeches (black, olive, red, yellow, rust), Woolly Bugger, Scud, Waterboatman, Borger's Snail, Prince, Pheasant Tail, Olive Flashback Hare's Ear, Bloodworm, Carey Specials, Damsel, Sparkle Pupa, Soft Hackle Hare's Ear, large Gold-Ribbed Hare's Ear.

When to Fish
Fishing is usually good after ice-out, which begins in May. June and July are the best months, but don't overlook the rest of the season, especially evenings.

Season & Limits
Open all year, but ice dictates when you can fish. Catch & release barbless hooks only.

1 Warm Springs boat launch. Access is good for a mile upstream along highway.

2 Popular camp & day use area.

3 End of easy float from Warm Springs or begin the challenging float to Maupin.

4 A very good camp & day use area. Popular with steelheaders in October.

5 Only accessible by boat. Great trout fishing.

6 Super spot for the "off" season.

Middle Deschutes River

Types of Fish
Predominantly redband rainbow trout with steelhead, some browns, bull trout & whitefish.

Flies to Use
Dry: Adams, Elk Hair Caddis, Blue Wing Olive, Slow Water Caddis, Henryville, CDC Caddis, Knock Down Dun, Clark's Stone, March Brown, Griffith's Gnat, X Caddis, Comparadun, Pale Morning Dun, Renegade, Salmon Flies and October Caddis.
Nymph: Girdle Bug, Hare's Ear, Kaufmann's Stone, Sparkle Pupa, Feather Duster, Bead Head Pheasant Tail, Prince, Brassie, October Caddis Pupa, Yellow Soft Hackle, Bead Head Serendipity. In late winter use #14 to #18 Black Stone.

When to Fish
Trout fish whenever you can. Evening fishing, in the summer, is the best time.

Season & Limits
Seasons and limits vary and are subject to frequent changes. Consult the ODFW synopsis or a local fly shop before fishing. Generally, trout and steelhead fish during the traditional trout season on the mid to lower sections. Return all wild steelhead.

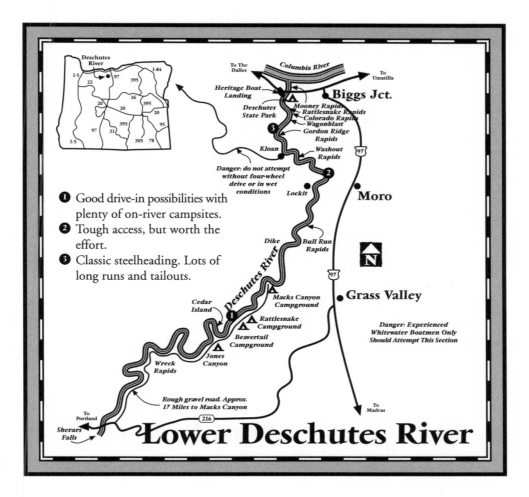

Lower Deschutes River

Types of Fish

Predominantly hatchery-reared steelhead, which have one or more fins clipped for identification. Current regulations allow you to keep hatchery fish only. Let the wild steelhead go unharmed. Also redband trout and whitefish.

Flies to Use

Steelhead: Sparsely tied "low water" patterns are best in purple, black and orange. Purple Peril, Freight Train, Green Butt Skunk, Skunk, Red Wing Blackbird, Mack's Canyon. Weighted flies include Purple Flash, Articulated Leech, Lead Eye Egg Sucking-Woolly Bugger, Girdle Bug, Beadhead Prince.

When to Fish

Usually late July - October is best up to Mack's Canyon. August - November is great, Mack's Canyon to Sherars Falls. Late September - October, Sherars Falls to Warm Springs.

1 Heavy water, limited fishing, nice fish.
2 Bridge 99. Road ends, hike or bike.
3 Good section of the river, requires walking.
4 Wizard Falls Fish Hatchery.
5 Good fishing, Canyon Creek to hatchery.
6 Heavily fished but you'll like it.
7 Allingham Bridge.
8 Lots of people.
9 Nice wild fish, Camp Sherman to Lake Creek.
10 Headwaters of the Metolius, spawning area, tread lightly.

Metolius River

Types of Fish

Rainbows, browns, whitefish plus bull trout that average 3 to 5 pounds.

Flies to Use

Dry: Sparkle, Captive & Knock Down Dun, Comparadun, Baetis, Pale Morning Dun, Green Drake, Cinygmula, Mahogany Dun, Pale Evening Dun. Elk Hair, Henryville, Slow Water and X-Caddis. Clark's Stone, Sofa Pillow, Stimulator, Yellow Sally, Adams.

Nymph: Beadhead Pheasant Tail, Prince or Flashback. Hare's Ear, Zug Bug, Golden Stone, October Caddis, Soft Hackle.

Streamer: Sculpin, White Rabbit Leech.

When to Fish

The river fishes pretty well year around. Excellent action November through March. Best results seem to be after 9:30 AM.

Seasons & Limits

Fly fishing only from Bridge 99 upstream to the private property boundary near the walk-in campgrounds. Winter, fly fishing only below Allingham Bridge. No boats or tubes. Check the ODFW synopsis for special regulations.

Metolius River Hatch Chart

	January	February	March	April	May	June
Baetis Mayfly	░	▓	░			
Midges		▓	░			
Tiny Speckled Stone			▓	░		
Stripe Wing Caddis	░					
October Caddis						
Speckled Wing Caddis			░	▓	░	
Spring Caddis				▓	▓	
Yellow/Olive Mayfly				▓	▓	▓
Green Drake					▓	▓
Golden Stone						
Mid-Size Mayflies				░	▓	
Micro Caddis						
Midges						
Late Evening Caddis						
Tiny Green Stone						
Pale Stone						
Fall Green Drake						
October Caddis						
Baetis Mayfly						
Yellow/Olive Mayfly						

	July	August	September	October	November	December
Baetis Mayfly						
Midges						
Tiny Speckled Stone						
Stripe Wing Caddis						
October Caddis						
Speckled Wing Caddis						
Spring Caddis						
Yellow/Olive Mayfly	▓					
Green Drake						
Golden Stone	▓	▓	░			
Mid-Size Mayflies	▓	░				
Micro Caddis		▓				
Midges						
Late Evening Caddis		▓	▓			
Tiny Green Stone	░					
Pale Stone		▓	▓			
Fall Green Drake						
October Caddis			░	▓	▓	
Baetis Mayfly				▓	░	
Yellow/Olive Mayfly						

Times and places of insect hatches change from season to season. This is especially true on the Metolius. This hatch chart is a good, but rough and preliminary guide to the months one typically finds various insects hatching on the Metolius.

Common Fly Fishing Terms

Dun
The stage of a mayfly's development just after it has emerged and has the ability to fly.

Emerger
That stage in the development of a water-borne insect when it leaves its shuck and emerges into a flying insect.

Fry
A baby fish.

Hatch
The time when a species of waterborne insect is emerging and becoming a flying insect.

Lake Trout
Not real trout, a member of the Char family. They not only live in lakes, they also spawn there.

Leader
A thin, clear monofilament tapered line attached to the end of the fly line, to which either the tippet or fly is attached.

Mayfly
(Order Ephemeroptera) A very common waterborne insect characterized by wings held in a nearly vertical position

Midge
(Order Diptera) A very small, mosquito-type fly often imitated by fly tiers.

Nymph
An undeveloped insect. Nymphs live underwater prior to emerging into a winged insect.

Pool
A location in a stream where the water is deeper and runs slower.

Rainbow Trout
(Oncorhynchus mykiss) Trout, indigenous to Pacific drainages of the Rocky Mountains. Known for the rich, pinkish colors along the centerline.

Rise
A fish coming to the surface and feeding on some food source.

Run
A location in a stream characterized by deep running water over a rocky streambed.

Salmon
A large member of the salmonidae fish family that hatch in fresh water and migrate to a lake or the ocean. Most return to the stream of their origin to spawn and then die.

Sea Run
A term applied to trout that hatch in fresh water, then migrate to the sea to grow to adulthood, then return to their natal waters to spawn.

Spinner

The final stage during the mating session, when an insect falls, fatigued, to the water and dies.

Spinner Fall

That time when many thousands of insects like Mayflies fall to the water in their last mortal stage.

Spring Creek

A stream that originates from water coming up from the ground, as opposed to a freestone stream that originates from run-off or snow melt.

Steelhead

A type of rainbow trout that migrates from the stream or river in which it hatched to the ocean or a large, landlocked lake.

Stocker

A fish born and raised in a hatchery and then placed in a stream, river or lake for sport fishing.

Stonefly

(Order Plecoptera) A large aquatic insect that emerges by crawling out of the water, then splits its shuck and becomes a flying insect.

Streamer

A fly that imitates a small fish, worm, leech, etc.

Strike Indicator

A floating substance, most commonly foam or yarn, attached to the leader above the fly.

Structure

Large objects in a stream or lake, such as big rocks, trees, dock pilings, etc., around which fish stay.

Tail Out

A location in a stream at the end of a pool, where it again becomes shallow, fast-moving water over a rocky or sandy bottom.

Terrestrial

A fly that imitates an insect not born in the water, e.g. grasshopper, cricket, ant, or beetle.

Tippet

Very thin, monofilament material added to the end of a leader to extend the length or to rebuild the leader after tippet has been broken off or used up tying knots.

Trout

A member of the salmonids fish family.

Wet Fly

A fly fished below or in the surface film of water.

Wild

Fish born in the waters in which they are found, not raised in a hatchery.

Definitions adapted from The Easy Field Guide to Fly-Fishing Terms & Tips by David Phares. For the complete list of terms, tips and some humor send $2.00 to: Primer Publishers 5738 North Central Avenue Phoenix, Arizona 85012

Other No Nonsense Titles

Business Traveler's Guide To Fly Fishing The Western States

Seasoned road warrior Bob Zeller reveals where one can fly fish within a two hour drive from every major airport in thirteen western states.
ISBN #1-892469-01-4

Traveling on business (or for some other reason)? Turn drudgery into a fun fly fishing outing. Here's how to pack, what to tell the boss and what to expect. Lots of detailed, two color maps show where to go and how to get there.

With to-the-point facts and humor Bob's 30 years of fly fishing-while-on-the-road are your guide to exploring the outdoors, not just a hotel lobby or airport lounge.

A Woman's No Nonsense Guide To Fly Fishing Favorite Waters

A First In Fly Fishing Guidebooks!
ISBN #1-892469-03-0

Forty-five of the top women fly fishing experts reveal their favorite waters. From scenic spring creeks in the East, big trout waters in the Rockies to exciting Baja, Florida and Northeast saltwater: all described from the distinctive female perspective. A major donation from each printing will go to Casting For Recovery, a non-profit organization that assists women recovering from breast cancer.

Taylor Streit's No Nonsense Guide To Fly Fishing In New Mexico

The San Juan, Cimarron, Gila, Chama, Rio Grande, mountain lakes and more.
ISBN #0-9637256-6-1

The first all inclusive guide to the top fly fishing waters in the Land of Enchantment. Since 1970 Mr. Streit has been THE New Mexico fly fishing authority and #1 professional guide. He developed many fly patterns used throughout the region, owned the Taos Fly Shop for ten years and managed a bone fishing lodge in the Bahamas. He makes winter fly fishing pilgrimages to Argentina where he escorts fly fishers and explores.

Gary Graham's No Nonsense Guide To Fly Fishing Southern Baja

With this book you can fly to Baja, rent a car and go out on your own to find exciting saltwater fly fishing!
ISBN #1-892469-00-6

Mexico's Baja Peninsula is now one of the premier destinations for saltwater fly anglers. Here's the latest and best information from Baja fly fishing authority, Gary Graham. This Orvis endorsed guide has over 20 years of Baja fishing experience. He operates *Baja on the Fly*, a top guiding operation located in Baja's famed "East Cape" region.

Bill Mason's
No Nonsense Guide
To Fly Fishing In Idaho

The Henry's Fork, Salmon, Snake and Silver Creek plus 24 other waters.
ISBN #0-9637256-1-0

Mr. Mason penned the first fly fishing guidebook to Idaho in 1994. It was updated in 1996 and showcases Bill's 30 plus years of Idaho fly fishing experience.

Bill helped build a major outfitting operation at the Henry's Fork and helped open the first fly shop in Boise. In Sun Valley he developed the first fly fishing school and guiding program at Snug Fly Fishing. Bill eventually purchased the shop, renaming it Bill Mason Outfitters.

Jackson Streit's
No Nonsense Guide
To Fly Fishing In Colorado

The Colorado, Rio Grande, Platte, Gunnison, mountain lakes and more.
ISBN #0-9637256-4-5

Mr. Streit fly fished Colorado for over 28 years and condensed this experience into a guidebook, published in 1995 and updated, improved and reprinted in 1997.

Jackson started the first guide service in the Breckenridge area and in 1985 he opened the region's first fly shop, The Mountain Angler, which he owns and manages.

Harry Teel's
No Nonsense Guide
To Fly Fishing In Central
and Southeastern Oregon

New. Updated & Reprinted.
The Metolius, Deschutes, McKenzie, Owyhee, John Day & 35 other waters.
ISBN #1-892469-09-X

Mr. Teel combined his 60 years of fly fishing into the first No Nonsense fly fishing guide. It was published in 1993 and updated, expanded and improved in 1998 by Jeff Perin. Jeff owns and operates the Fly Fisher's Place, the premier fly shop in Sisters, Oregon originally started by Mr. Teel.

Ken Hanley's
No Nonsense Guide
To Fly Fishing In California

New. Spring 2003
ISBN #1-892469-10-3

Mr. Hanley and some very talented contributors like Jeff Solis, Dave Stanley, Katie Howe and others, have fly fished nearly every top water in California. Saltwater, bass, stealhead, high mountains, they provide all you need to discover the best places to fly fish in the Golden State.

Steve Schmidt's
No Nonsense Guide
To Fly Fishing Utah

Every fly angler has heard of the famed Green River, but the rest of Utah yields extraordinary, uncrowded and little known fishing.
ISBN #0-9637256-8-8

Steve Schmidt, outfitter and owner of Western Rivers Fly Shop in Salt Lake City has explored these waters for over 27 years. He explains where to go and how to fish some of the most unique and diverse waters in the west. There's something for everybody, fly fishing mountain streams and lakes, tailwaters, bass waters and reservoirs.

Glenn Tinnin's
No Nonsense Guide
To Fly Fishing Arizona

If you are visiting the many scenic wonders of the Grand Canyon State, or moving there, bring your fly rod and this guidebook!
ISBN 1892469-02-2

Arizona has both famous and little known fishing. Waters flow through desert, forest, lava fields, red rocks and canyons. Glenn Tinnin, outfitter and guide has explored these waters for over 20 years. He explains where to go and how to fish 32 fly fishing waters including mountain streams and lakes, bass waters, reservoirs and saltwater fly fishing at Rocky Point, Mexico, a favorite and nearby getaway for Phoenix-Area anglers.

Dave Foster's
Guide To Fly Fishing
Lee's Ferry, Arizona

A clear understanding of the complex and fascinating 15 miles of the Colorado River below Glenn Canyon Dam.
ISBN 1-892469-07-3

Detailed maps direct fly and spin fishing and show points of history, boating and geologic landmarks and access to the natural history and beauty. Indispensable for the angler and intrepid visitor to the Marble Canyon. Includes fold-out map.

For over 20 years author Dave Foster has boated, explored and guided anglers on the big water that courses below the huge sandstone cliffs that start the Grand Canyon. His passion for the history and fishing in Lees Feery is a huge step forward in the ongoing chronicle of the fascinating river and crossing.

Terry Barron's
No Nonsense Guide
To Fly Fishing Pyramid Lake
Nevada

The Gem of the Desert is full of huge Lahontan Cutthroat trout.
ISBN #0-9637256-3-7

Mr. Barron is the Reno-area and Pyramid Lake fly fishing guru. He helped establish the Truckee River Fly Fishers Club and ties and works for the Reno Fly Shop.

Terry has recorded the pertinent information to fly fish the most outstanding trophy cutthroat fishery in the U.S. Where else can you get tired of catching 18-25" trout?

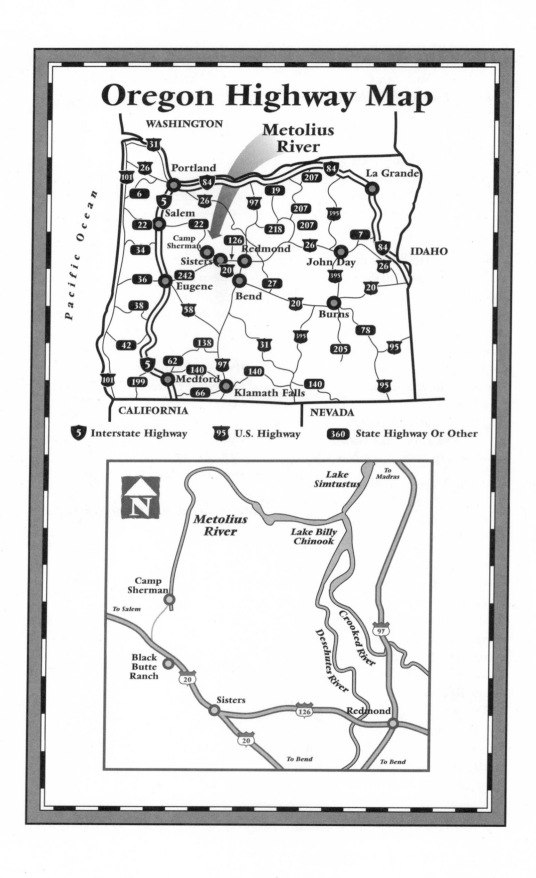

Oregon Highway Map

Metolius River

WASHINGTON

Pacific Ocean

31
26
101
6
5
22
34
36
38
42
5
199
101

Portland
84
26
22
Salem
22
Camp Sherman
Sisters
242
Eugene
58
62
140
Medford
66

84
207
19
97
218
126
Redmond
20
27
Bend
20
138
31
97
140
140
Klamath Falls

La Grande
84
207
207
207
395
7
26
John Day
395
20
Burns
395
205
78
95
95
84
26
20

IDAHO

NEVADA

CALIFORNIA

5 Interstate Highway **95** U.S. Highway **360** State Highway Or Other

N

Metolius River

Lake Simtustus
To Madras

Lake Billy Chinook

Camp Sherman
To Salem

Crooked River

Deschutes River

97

Black Butte Ranch
20

Sisters
126
Redmond

20

To Bend

To Bend

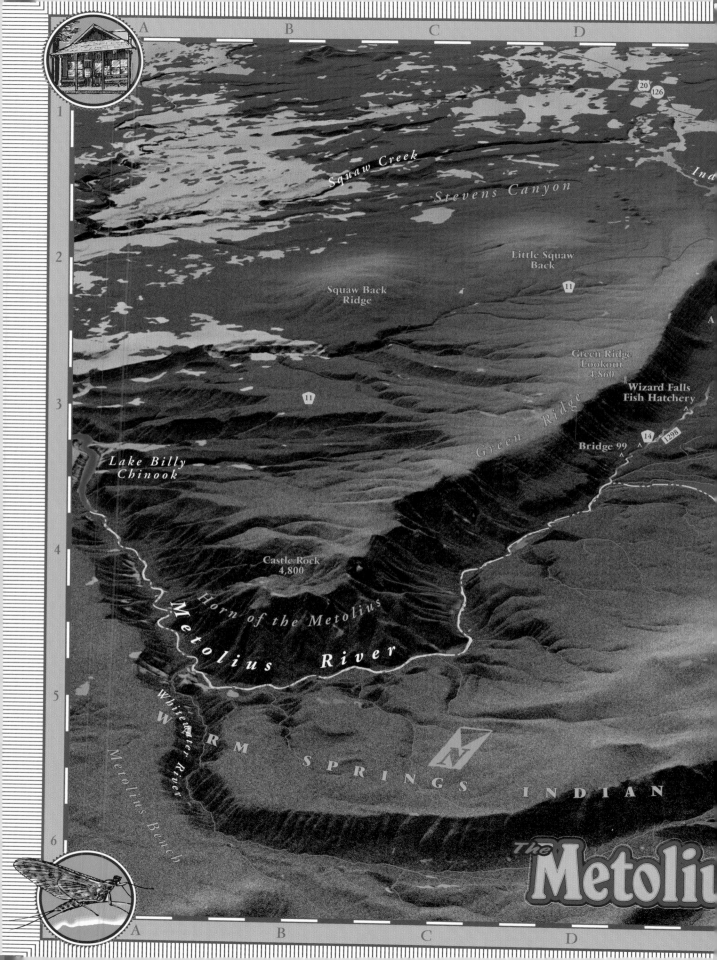

The Metoliu

Sisters

an Ford Creek

Black Butte
Ranch

Black Crater
7,251

Mt. Washington
7,794

Black Butte
6,436

Head of
The Metolius

14

Suttle
Lake

Camp
herman

1419

20 126

ngham
ridge

1419

1216

Lake Creek

1217

Jack Creek

Three Finger
Jack,
7,841

1420

Canyon Creek

bbott Creek

Candle Creek

Jefferson Creek Lava Flow

Jefferson Creek

Mt. Jefferson
10,497

RESERVATION

s River
Basin